THE THIRD SPACE

A Nonconformist's Guide to the Universe

ZANDER KEIG

THE THIRD SPACE

Hardcover ISBN: 978-1-61343-168-9

Paperback ISBN: 978-1-61343-169-6

Ebook ISBN: 978-1-61343-170-2

This book is dedicated to: my late father, Ricardo Alberto Hermelin, who taught me so much about living a good life and how to be a good person; my wife, Margaret Keig, who has loved me unconditionally for twenty-two years; my mentor, Dr. Jamison Green, who has generously shared his wisdom and time with me along my transition journey the last nineteen years; and the friends, there are too many to name, who have enriched my life over the years.

In February of 2022, I flew from Washington, DC, to Miami to attend a national gathering of an organization of which I am on the Board of Advisors.

I had been instructed to download an app to my phone and enter a specific code to bill my ground transportation to the organization. A glitch occurred, and I paid out of pocket to travel from the airport to the hotel where the gathering was taking place. Not wishing to continue paying out of pocket for additional ground transportation, I sought help from anyone with tech knowledge who might understand how to fix the problem with my app. Several people I asked were experiencing the same problem, while others whose apps worked fine could not resolve my issue.

Then I met Zander Keig, another Board Advisor. Like the others, he was initially perplexed by the problem, but unlike them, he was undeterred and defiant to the idea of allowing this phone app to defeat him. Not only did he fix the problem, but he explained what had happened and voluntarily took the time to teach me how to fix it without uninstalling and reinstalling it should it happen again.

The overture of kindness, perseverance, and generosity in imparting knowledge by this man has led to a friendship I would not trade for anything in the world.

Zander Keig is what I would consider to be nothing short of a master locksmith. He has the lockpicking and decoding skills to open and reset the tumblers and combination number codes to the secrets of living life to the fullest in the face of discrimination, rejection, locked doors, and various obstacles placed upon life's pathways and journeys.

He seeks contentment by being challenged but is not content by winning, only by pursuing the next challenge. Zander is a lifelong student of learning and is equally comfortable as a teacher sharing his expertise and wealth of knowledge with others.

'The Third Space: A Nonconformist's Guide To The Universe' turns every reader into an expert locksmith by providing them with the ultimate master key that unlocks the doors they once thought were shut to them in their lives. Armed with empirical lifelong experiences combined with academic master degrees in Conflict Analysis & Resolution, Clinical Social Work, and Theology, Zander Keig has transformed the lives of countless individual U.S. veterans and improved the productivity of corporations by training thousands of employees as well as some of their trainers.

As a small child just a few years out of the womb, Zander defied the odds, and with sheer determination, survived a bad allergic reaction to a vaccine that put him in a coma and almost took his life. After this left him with various afflictions, he suffered bullying but went on to join the U.S. military and proudly served his country. Overcoming contemplations of suicide and despair, he met every conceivable challenge and adversity life threw at him head-on with various transitions, both emotional and physical, along the way to successfully transforming himself into one of the most incredible human beings and friends I have ever had the pleasure of meeting.

This book is not so much about Zander's transitions through life as it is about his remarkable ability to transform every negative experience into a positive learning experience, which has propelled him into the happiest and most successful time of his life, with more to come.

This is an enjoyable page-turner that touches every emotion known to man as Zander becomes your lifelong partner and teacher, taking you on a journey through his incredible life. Along the way, you will see many similarities and obstacles in your own life. He will empower you with your own master key and lock-pick kit as you learn to unlock your incredible potential and navigate the destiny you have chosen for yourself and not one with which others attempt to force you to comply.

– Daryl Davis

Daryl Davis is a musician, race reconciliator, and the author of 'Klan-Destine Relationships – A Black Man's Odyssey In The Ku Klux Klan' and 'The Klan Whisperer – Sitting At MLK's Table Of Brotherhood'.

TABLE OF CONTENTS

INTRODUCTION

INTRODUCTION

When I was six years old, before I started first grade, my mother took me to the doctor to get the MMR vaccine for measles, mumps, and rubella.

Unfortunately, it was a bad batch, and I contracted rubella, the German measles. The virus went into my brain and caused some swelling, called encephalitis.

I spent a few months in the hospital. During that time, I was in a medically induced coma for two weeks because I was having seizures, and they were worried they would destroy the muscles in my body.

When I regained consciousness after the coma, I was paralyzed on the left side of my body, and I was blind in my left eye. So my parents and the doctors had to figure out what the next steps would be.

Back at school two years later, I was teased because I had a limp from the paralysis that I had overcome at this point. Not only was I told that I had an "Arizona accent" when I moved to California, but since the left side of my face had been paralyzed, it affected the way I spoke.

I was bullied, I was teased, and I was pushed around both physically and verbally.

After about two years, I decided I had enough. I started fighting back against the bullies, and other kids around me noticed.

They would approach me and say, "Hey, so-and-so is picking on me. They're pushing me, and they're calling me names."

I would go over to those bullies, and I would bully them because I didn't want other kids to have to experience the kind of bullying I had experienced.

It tears down your sense of self, and it destroys

your spirit. When we treat people that way, especially children, it can have a lifelong impact on their sense of being in the world as they go through life.

Years later, I was telling someone that story, and they gave me the nickname of 'Robin Hood bully'.

I have to tell you, I have never really outgrown that. To this day, I consider myself the Robin Hood bully because I do not tolerate bullies.

I don't care if it's in the workplace, in my neighborhood, among my social network, on television, or in Congress; it doesn't matter. I don't take kindly to bullies.

It's important to note that I was a woman until age 39. Now I'm a trans man. It was 20 years ago that I began the process of medically transitioning.

During my middle school years, I wasn't in a traditional middle school. I was actually sent away to a group home for delinquent girls. It was an all-girls residential school.

I was 14 years old and at a point in life where I was struggling with the transition from childhood to adolescence.

A childhood that I didn't really get to live because I was sick for so much of it. But like a child, I was an optimist, and I'm still an optimist. I believed that people were inherently good, life has its positives, and things have a way of working out. I still hold that belief.

Furthermore, in my late teens, I ended up in a relationship with a woman who was very abusive, physically and mentally. It destroyed me more than anything else in my life up to that point.

After two years, I was looking for a way to escape. The options I provided to myself were: suicide, joining the military, or committing a heinous crime that would send me away to prison, so I'd never have to see her again. It was really drastic, but I felt like I was at the end of my rope.

In some ways, I didn't have the protective factors or the protective layers that kept me from entering into that kind of relationship.

I just fell right into it because I lacked the awareness to recognize the signs and traits associated with such people.

However, I made it through and ended up going

into the military. I completed basic training, which lasted 12 weeks, rather than the usual 10 weeks.

I did the third week of basic training three times. What that means is that I failed, and then I failed again.

And why did I fail? Because I was rebellious and being defiant towards my commanding officer, they kept reverting me, pushing me back, to a new company.

I finally ended up in the third company, and I had a very stern but kind drill instructor. I was 20 years old, and everyone else was 18 or 19. Despite my issues, he recognized I had leadership qualities, so he gave me the benefit of the doubt and made me a company officer.

I spent the rest of my time in basic training without a single infraction.

Along the way, people believed in me and gave me the benefit of the doubt. This gave me something to hold on to for a better possibility for myself in the future.

I think I have to backtrack a little by saying that my father introduced me to Transcendental Meditation when I was 12. And since then, different forms of meditation have been a big factor in my life.

At that time, as a child, I practiced a walking form of meditation. But I've also learned different sitting forms of meditation and others, like the Vietnamese Buddhist Thích Nhất Hanh's mindful dishwashing, which is one of my favorite forms of mindfulness practice.

I have faced many challenges, and I've overcome them, and a lot of it is due to meditation, mindfulness, and a few people believing in me and giving me different opportunities.

But I've also done it by following a path that offers a 'third space'.

For example, I'm not a theist or an atheist. I'm a non-theist.

I'm not a Democrat or a Republican. I'm an Independent.

I've walked this path my entire life, always finding that middle way, the middle space.

Even before I started my medical transition, whenever I went to an event where they would divide the room into men and women, I would always stand in the middle of the room.

I would assert that I was going to stay in the middle of the room, and anyone who wanted to join me could.

I just insisted that there was likely a middle way in every situation I found myself in.

I've been able to figure out from navigating this middle path that it attracts negative attention from those who take sides; the left and the right, the believers and the non-believers.

As a result, I've had to find ways to create a protective shield around myself. I've done that by learning how to manage the strong reactions that are coming from people through developing emotion regulation.

I've learned how to stand still in situations where people are furious with me for something that I've said and just be in that space without it impacting me. That's called distress tolerance.

I've also learned how to navigate difficult conversations with people applying conflict management techniques, that bring people out of debate and into dialogue.

I've learned that life is inevitably going to be filled with challenges that are bound to affect us physically and psychologically.

I want to share with you how to learn to do what I've done. For example, how to regulate emotions, tolerate distress, mitigate conflict, and manage stress.

I've learned that the world is not going to change to meet my needs.

I'm not saying we have to change ourselves entirely to meet the needs of society. However, we can find this third space, and discover what we do and don't want to change about ourselves, and then strengthen ourselves, so we can walk that path and not be destroyed by people's response to it.

Go the way of the Buddha, the middle path. Buddhism is the middle path between Hinduism and Jainism as experienced by the Buddha.

In Taoism, there's this principle for determining if something is seen as good or bad, the wise Taoist would listen to the concerns of others, shrug his shoulders and say, "Maybe, maybe not."

Taoists strive to live in that uncertainty, or what they call "the unknowing."

That's a very uncomfortable thing in Western culture. Unknowing? Uncertainty? We do not like that, but we can learn to accept it, and in some cases, I think we can grow to appreciate it.

I actually appreciate uncertainty and unknowing because it gives me more space to wonder.

If I'm not certain about something, and I'm not entirely uncertain, I've moved into curiosity, wondering, looking, asking, recognizing, or listening.

That place between certainty and uncertainty is the unknowing, or it can be the curious place.

I like being curious.

Perhaps that's the child in me, because children are naturally curious.

We tend to lose a sense of curiosity unless we go into a profession where it's a big advantage, like science. Scientists get really curious in their pursuit of knowledge.

Can you recall a time in your life when you faced a challenge and overcame it?

Most people can say that has happened. That's because you're capable of it. You're capable of facing challenges and overcoming them.

People lose sight of their capabilities because they're so far underwater that they forget that all they have to do is come up for air. Or they're in the shallow end, so they just have to stand up.

There are certain things that happen in our lives which we have no control.

But we do have control over how we respond to those situations.

I'm pretty sure every single one of you is experiencing challenges right now. Read on, if you'd like to find a way to deal with them differently.

– Zander Keig, March 2024

CHAPTER 1

ESCAPIST

The ability to think things through does not come naturally to everyone. It is often influenced by their worldview, schooling, and family.

We get locked in our mindset, how we interact with people, preconceived notions about things, and our beliefs and identity.

We get trapped in expectations, and we get trapped in the past. Our relationships, fears, or regrets can also serve as gilded cages, keeping us confined.

We can get trapped in silos, which might be the case for some people who want to do a particular job, and then do it for 50 or 60 years until they retire.

Other people bounce around, but I've met so many people who don't really know what they want to be when they grow up, and they're already grown up. We might get trapped in occupational or friend network silos, and we don't really go outside of them.

It might only be temporary, and we might like our silos, but we don't know that until we actually check them out.

I was recently listening to a podcast, and they said something that really hit home for me: there's the trap and there's the escape.

How do we escape?

I was reminded of a webinar I teach all the time that has this concept called radical acceptance. It's part of building resilience and emotional intelligence.

I said, "That's it. That's what sets you free. Radical acceptance of what is."

It's not that you succumb to it or just let it all happen, but you give up fighting it and work on figuring out how to get out of it. You find out how to make it work because being trapped is all in your head.

A trap is a mental or emotional limitation that either seems or maybe is externally placed upon us. It can also be placed internally.

This is related to the concept of learned helplessness. This is a fascinating phenomenon where people are denied, up to a certain point in their life, the ability to do things for themselves.

Then, when they're confronted with, "Here, do this thing. You can do it," and if they don't believe they are able to ... they have succumbed to the constraints of their circumstances.

Because they don't trust themselves and don't believe that they're capable of doing it, they get trapped in their helplessness.

The feeling of not trusting that you can do it.

They're afraid of failing.

They don't understand that failure is the predominant experience in life. People are trying to avoid and escape from failure, which is not possible.

There's another trap you can fall into when you try to escape pain and failure. The trap that gets placed on us is internal.

We are free to move about, but we limit ourselves internally. This extends to what we believe we are capable of doing with our access to the external, physical world.

It's the acceptance piece, this radical acceptance of failing, getting hurt, losing, or whatever it is.

Some people are also afraid of actually succeeding because once you achieve success, you think, "Oh, shit. Now people are going to expect this from me."

We get trapped in that too.

This radical acceptance of failure is similar to when we were learning to ride a bike as kids.

We got back up, dusted ourselves off, hopped on the bike, and rode again. We fell again, and the process kept repeating, and we kept falling until we didn't.

Hopefully, we had someone tender and nurturing teaching us how to ride a bike. Or sometimes, you could have someone like my dad who said, "Stop falling. Get on the bike."

It all depends on the temperament of the person who's teaching you how to ride a bike, drive a car, or tell the time on the clock.

Is it under duress, like mine was, pulled off on the side of the road because I couldn't tell the time on the clock with little hands and no numbers inside the car when I was 10?

It was pretty alarming, thinking back. I was in the car with my father, and we were driving somewhere.

I asked him, "What time is it?" or "What time do we need to be there?" Just something about the time.

He instructed me to tell him what time it was on the clock in the car.

We were in a 1970s car, so it didn't have a digital clock. Like most old watches, it just had little lines with moving hands. No numbers or Roman numerals.

I couldn't tell the time.

I had been taught how to tell time using a clock with numbers on it. I was 10, and I was in the 5th grade. I mean, I theoretically knew how to tell time, but there had to be numbers on the clock.

Thank goodness we were on just some side road and not on the freeway because my dad pulled over and wouldn't move until I could tell the time. I was forced to figure out how to tell the time on the spot.

He moved the dial and asked, "What time is it?"

He moved it again and asked what time it was. I was under a lot of pressure.

I was learning how to tell time while trapped in the car.

I found myself trapped in a car with my father several times, actually, and he would get really angry.

He would ball up his fist and pound it on my left leg, the one closest to him. I thought of jumping out of the car on a few occasions. I did not, but I remember wanting to open the door and just tumble out.

I remember recounting this story to my father before he got dementia, and asking him if he remembered it. He had no recollection of it.

That is an example of a physical and a mental trap I endured.

If I were to think about the first moment I was trapped, I don't have a conscious memory of this, but I would say it was when my mother was pregnant with me.

I've heard this story from my grandparents and parents, so I trust it's true.

My mother was told I was dead.

The doctors told her they were going to take me out because they couldn't hear my heartbeat.

She was only seven months pregnant.

They did a surgical procedure, cutting open the belly, and then when they pulled me out they must have tested me again because they said I had a faint heartbeat.

For two months, I was put in an incubator. It was a little plastic coffin-like box with oxygen pumping into it, which in the 1960s could have been hazardous.

Maybe being in the belly and presumed dead wasn't a trap. Being put in an incubator?

That's kind of a form of being trapped.

———

Being two months premature isn't a big deal now, but it was in the 60s. People talked about it like it was almost a miracle that I survived.

It's the same with the incubator: I came out of it okay, not with any blindness or vision loss, which was something that used to happen. I had no cognitive deficits.

But then, when I was six, I got encephalitis, which led to paralysis. And as a paralyzed person, I was trapped in a hospital bed. I don't recall this story exactly because I was too little and had brain damage.

However, my parents told me that the doctors were shocked that I was doing as well as I was. My mother told me the doctors said it was because I was so stubborn.

I'm sure they described me as something different from that, like belligerent, aggressive, or whatever it was. I not only overcame the paralysis but the vision issue in my left eye got corrected with glasses.

I was even able to go into the military, so the paralysis and the vision issues didn't stop me from succeeding in that venue.

I don't know exactly what the fuel was for that escape, the route, or the energy behind it. I must be very fortunate.

Perhaps it's a miracle, who knows? I remember enough in my memory that I hold onto it.

I know, "Oh, I've been through that, I've been through all these things."

So that gives me the knowledge that I can escape, or make it through. I can overcome it. I can exceed people's expectations.

I can get out of those traps.

Two things come to mind when thinking about how I exceeded expectations when I was younger.

One was a 'fuck you' energy.

The other is a bit abstract. It's a strong will to live.

It's a sense of, 'I have to, I want to, I need to.

I'm destined for something.'

I kind of felt that from a really young age.

When I heard the stories of what happened to me really early in my life, I thought, "I'm supposed to be here."

Who the hell goes through all of that for no reason?

I even had an alcohol overdose. I pulled a classic '60s rock star thing where I vomited in my mouth while lying on my back. I could have died.

There've been so many times in my life where I've almost died, and so I think, "I must be here for something."

I'm not sure what it is yet.

So here is a list of traps. Things we are trapped by. Things that we believe we can't get out of.

Or rather, things we can get out of. We just might need to ask for help or try a little harder.

Non-Reality Trap

I have been on the receiving end of people be-lieving what others have said about me, pros and cons, both of which can be difficult to deal with.

I've been the victim of rumors, gossip, defa-mation, and slander. It continues to this day. There's a legal issue going on where lawyers have sent a cease and desist letter because this one individual who just won't leave me alone.

They post things about me that aren't true all over social media. People who don't know me well enough or at all, take it as truth.

Why do they believe this person is telling the truth? Because they fit certain identity cate-gories of the type of people that you're always supposed to believe.

Supposedly, I don't fit into those categories, but they don't know me. Their different iden-tities are deemed to fit some mold that makes them more believable than me.

People are making up their minds based on something someone has said.

Then they're telling everyone else who I am according to their belief that's coming from hearsay. It's hard to get out of that trap.

It's a kind of trap that I've experienced over and over again.

I talked to someone not too long ago and they said, "Why do you think that keeps happening to you?"

I told them I wasn't sure, and they said, "Well, maybe people are envious because you have a level of success that they don't have."

Well, maybe.

But here's what I know. Believing things about people without knowing them creates a rupture where there is potential for friendship.

This person and I have a lot of things in common. We'd probably be friends, or at least friendly. We live on opposite sides of the country now, but we used to live in the same city.

That's how I met them. We are both clinicians, we're both trans, and we're both trainers, educators, and speakers.

We have a lot in common.

I was talking to someone about this yesterday

because the cease and desist is in effect right now.

I said, "I'm not on TikTok, but I saw their image on their TikTok profile. They don't look well."

And the person I said this to said, "Why do you care?"

Well, they're a human being. I hope they're okay. They look so physically and emotionally unwell in the picture they put up.

It reminded me of a story I heard years ago about an anti-Semite who used to call a rabbi every week to say horrible things to him and then just hang up.

The rabbi realized at one point that he hadn't heard from the guy in a few weeks, so he called him to check up on him.

"Are you okay? I haven't heard from you." The guy was shocked. They developed a friendly relationship.

This story resonates with me because here's this person who has, nonstop for several years, been trying to go after companies that hire me.

One of those companies is now going after them.

I'm so thankful I didn't have to do it because I was worried about the repercussions of going after them directly.

This person seems furious and unhappy in the world. I'm not the only person they've gone after. They've spent so much time targeting people, being angry at people, slandering them, and destroying their reputations.

And why? For what? They have a job, and they have all this good work that they could be doing. Why aren't they focused on those things?

Anger limits people's ability to be their best selves. They're constantly caught up in trying to destroy other people's lives.

It's very limiting. I think it's bad for people's physical and emotional health because when you have a lot of anger, which produces tension in your body, you constrict your blood flow so much that you could deny your body and brain proper oxygen and nutrients.

That's not good.

Belief Trap

The belief trap is not just about having beliefs.

There are a lot of beliefs that people have, but we get stuck in them when we're unwilling to acknowledge that our belief system or the ideas we hold aren't fully formed.

There have been a lot of interactions over time, resulting in developing culture, philosophy, religion, art, music, and people becoming integrated.

Many religions have developed from earlier beliefs. For example, you can see how one religion was formed from a previous one, which led to the creation of another religion that acknowledged both original religions.

The Buddha said, "I don't want to be a Brahman in Hindu tradition and those Jains are too ascetic, so I'm going to create this new thing called Buddhism, right?"

I guess that's my GenX interpretation of Siddhartha's story.

Christianity also has elements of paganism in

it. It's just interesting to look at how a lot of different things influence other things.

But if we get stuck in a narrow belief about a religion, philosophy, person, or guru, that's similar to being in a cult.

That's what a cult is, right? A cult is a very narrow view or belief that this particular individual or belief system is the one that is the deliverer of the good news, so to speak.

The way out of the belief trap is testing the belief, but that's very difficult for a person to do because it's frightening.

If they discover that their belief is either wrong or not entirely what they believe it to be, then they are going to lose something.

They're going to lose a sense of comfort, a sense of belonging. They're going to lose a sense of feeling satisfied with whatever their belief is and this might end up with them leaving the group, which means leaving a lot behind, including friends and potentially a home.

In cults, you get cut off from your family and friends. As a result, they become the enemy. Slowly but surely, they have to be reminded that, hopefully, their parents aren't their enemy.

They show them a photograph and say, "Hey, remember this? Remember me?"

I mean, people could have abusive parents, but we hope that's not the case. The people who have abusive parents or those who don't have a family are the most vulnerable.

It is the introduction that is being chipped away at, or cracked into. It is shining a light on the belief that you have or the concept that has been presented to you that you have taken wholeheartedly as a belief.

It's either done in a small way or in a really big way.

The middle way isn't going to be as workable because it has to be something incrementally small to just get a person to think about things like, 'Oh, well, if that's not true, what else isn't true?'

Then things start to unravel. It could also be something really massive, such as the FBI raiding your compounds, and you're sort of forced into it.

But in the meantime, you're just going day

after day, believing your belief. Nothing really challenges your beliefs because you're surrounded by people and places reinforcing it.

You have to get outside the reinforcement, but it's not easy to do that.

I promise it will be worth it. Give that belief trap a little shake for me.

Expectation Trap

There are many expectations that we deal with in life.

There's the expectation that you are going to be born with 10 fingers and 10 toes and have perfect vision and hearing.

People often have this expectation that they're going to give birth to a perfect baby.

Babies are all perfect, but there are certain things that do happen. I was pronounced dead, and then I came out, and I was a preemie.

Then there's the expectation of how we should behave as children, as people.

People will say, "Well, we're not animals. We

have the sense to know what is right from wrong."

I believe most people or teachers expect a child to do well in school and get good grades.

We expect that the educators are truly enlightening our children.

We expect parents to raise children without coercive and abusive behaviors. (Sadly, we know it's not always true, or we wouldn't have child welfare services, right?)

At the end of the day, I think people who are just living with many expectations are disappointed a lot.

They're perpetually disappointed in everything.

That restaurant wasn't good enough.

That person wasn't good enough.

That movie wasn't good enough.

You hear people say this all the time, "It wasn't what I thought it would be. It wasn't what I expected."

To that, I say, "Well, you've never been here before. How did you manage to have an expectation of what it would be like?"

It's like they're constantly frustrated.

I mean, the simplest answer to get out of expectation traps is not to have them.

However, it's more complicated than that. I think expectations are imposed on us by the adults who have expectations.

My father was a big proponent of not having expectations in life.

Because of that, I inherited a mindset of challenging my expectations. Most people don't do that.

I'm rarely disappointed, and when I am, I say, "Oh, I had an expectation, and I let it go."

Sometimes it takes an outside force, like a person asking you nicely where that expectation came from. You have to figure out how to say it in a way that doesn't sound critical of the person.

I tend to do it by playing dumb. I say, "Oh, have you been here before?"

If they say they haven't, I tell them, "Oh, but somehow, you have an expectation about it."

I think most people think expectations are just natural. It might be for people who expect things all the time, but that's just because they're not aware that it's causing them to be disappointed all the time.

They just think they're always disillusioned because people aren't living up to their expectations.

Perhaps if you got rid of the expectations, you wouldn't be so disappointed all the time.

That's part of radical acceptance.

People are going to do things you don't want them to do, or they do them differently than you'd like them to do.

You might want to sever that friendship, or get a divorce, or leave the job, or whatever it is, because there's too much of it.

It's just about recognizing that you have an expectation.

I have an expectation that I've placed on this restaurant, this movie, this person, this job, this country, or this politician.

Therefore, I'm living as if they're not living up to my expectations. Well, why would they? There are over eight billion people in the world.

If we all had expectations, they'd all be very different, and no one could live up to all of them. It's like some kind of narcissistic trait.

It's not narcissism, but it's a trait of narcissism, just expecting the whole world to align with what you need, what you want, and what you expect.

Children are similar in that nature. It makes sense because they're still learning about the world. But it's no longer good when you're an adult and still like that.

Identity Trap

I had a Palestinian Muslim girlfriend for about three years. We met in college.

Her parents were both Israelis. Her mom was Jewish and Polish, and her dad was an Arab.

Her father was Muslim, but at that point, not fundamentalist in his beliefs. And then, something happened between her parents.

The three children got whisked off by their mom, changed their names, and lived in some compound, hiding from the father and his family.

They changed their names to Hebrew names

and went to a Hebrew school because they were Jewish kids. (Their mother was Jewish, so that made them also Jewish.)

Suddenly something happened again, and the father then took them away. Now, they were in an Islamic school with Arabic names. (And they were Muslim because their father was Muslim.)

Their father brought them to the United States. And their mother came soon after to watch over them. When we were together in college, for a whole year, I had no idea what was going on. She never told me. I was so confused.

She would leave school and go home, and there would be men there whom her father had invited over. Because he was trying to find her a husband, she was supposed to entertain them, serve them tea, and engage in conversation with them.

Her father told her that as soon as she graduated from college, she was going to have to marry one of these men.

She was just not having any of it. She would always do something, like spill tea or laugh with a snort on purpose, to dissuade the guy.

She'd do just anything to make her not be the

ideal, perfect wife.

Eventually, her father said, "When you finish college, I'm going to send you to Jordan. You're going to marry a cousin."

The day after graduation, we ran away to the Virgin Islands to escape her family. The night before, she told me what was going on in her family.

I had no idea that she had been a prisoner of her cultural identity at the hands of her father. She was trapped into being a proper Muslim woman, even with how she dressed and interacted with people.

She couldn't leave the house unless she was accompanied by her younger brother or an uncle.

It was humiliating for her.

I mean, think of that, in terms of an identity trap.

For me, I'd say that my identity traps had to do with expectations.

My maternal grandmother, who took care of me when my father was out of town, had expectations about how I should dress and behave; like a young lady.

I never did, so there was a lot of punishment because I wasn't behaving properly.

As a teenager, I continued to be very tomboyish because I hadn't outgrown it.

I was such a delinquent at that point, and I was doing things that got me in trouble.

I ended up being sent to a psychiatric institution for a year.

While I was there, they thought trying to make me more feminine would be a good idea. They put me through what they called 'fashion therapy.' I spent an entire year there.

They attempted to force me into behaving, dressing, and interacting with people in a feminine way.

Before that, my father never had those expectations. He was perfectly fine with me being a tomboy. I played soccer, I was very athletic. We lived by the beach, and I was there all the time. My dad just let me be a kid.

Only later, would I get teased about the way I

was dressed. And in the institution, I had expectations on how females should act forced onto me. Think about what that meant to me as a little girl, as a prepubescent girl, and then as a teenager, an adolescent girl, and even a young adult, a young woman.

So, I just went into the military. Of course, lots of women go into the military, but for me, it was a form of escape from this trap.

When I joined the military, I was also able to escape the societal expectations of how I dressed and the kind of work I did, because I was in a uniform that looked just like the men's uniform.

I was doing a job where I was right next to men doing the same mechanical kind of work and law enforcement primarily.

The gender trap is a little bit superimposed on that. The gender trap is my style of dressing, hairstyle, mannerisms, and the activities I engaged in that were not properly feminine.

You have the femaleness and the femininity there, sort of overlaying. I found my way into the lesbian community, where being a more masculine woman was not seen in a negative light. In fact, it was a positive thing in that community.

But whenever I was not in that community, not with my friends, just interacting with society, I had to deal with random stuff like "Effing dyke!" being yelled out of car windows.

It happened regularly enough that it's sort of etched in my mind. Then you have the more physical incidents of getting pushed and shoved.

Someone once even threw a bottle at my head when I was standing out on the street when I was still in the military.

People yelled, "faggots!" when we were standing outside a gay bar.

I was masculine enough that I think they thought I was a gay guy standing outside a gay bar.

They hurled bottles out the car window, and one of them smacked me right in the head. I was very androgynous, so sometimes people mistook me for a gay man and other times, a lesbian. That was always a fascinating phenomenon. Not very many people have that experience.

Particularly in the workplace, this started to become a problem. If I wanted to climb the ladder in the workplace, so to speak, there were expectations of how women should dress and interact with people in professional settings.

There are different levels of expectations, and I wasn't naturally doing those things.

A part of me just refused to do them and then, of course, the escape from that was to go to college and graduate school, where I could just wear my Vans tennis shoes and my shorts, T-shirts, or polo shirts.

Escape the identity trap. It will be worth it, even though you might have to go through some challenges, as I did.

Future Trap

Now here's a different kind of trap you might not be expecting me to talk about.

I talk about anxiety as due to a fear of some future event that is largely based on uncertainty.

Uncertainty is anxiety-producing for a lot of people because many like to be certain about things. They want to know, they want a definitive answer to a question. They want to be able to chart out their course. They want assurance that they're going to be able to get to where they want to go just by following this map.

There's always a lower level of uncertainty, but if it rises to the level of fear, it goes back to thoughts like, "What if I fail? What if I am wrong, or what if I don't know the answer?"

There are all these different fears. And the uncertainty of knowing how we'll do or what will be the outcome of something leads to anxiety.

If we can't stomp it down, it can even go beyond anxiety and into panic.

With a panic attack, everything speeds up. Our thoughts and heart rate increases, and we sweat profusely. We're not running, but we're sweating like we're running.

Our speech can speed up, and we start to speak really rapidly.

If you think of an even more extreme version of that, it would be a manic episode. If you've ever been around someone having a manic episode, they're going a mile a minute.

They don't even sleep for days at a time. They're completely psychotic and delusional while in this manic episode.

They're just going and going until they crash.

You might have uncertainties, but that's a given. We all have them, but it doesn't have to lead to fear and anxiety. It doesn't have to lead to that, but it does because people don't have the skills or the strategies to navigate through.

They don't have the toolkit to know how to deal with uncertainty, which includes, again, radical acceptance.

Mindfulness, slowing things down, thinking things through, breathing, and radical acceptance is all about saying, "Yeah, I'm not sure about this. This could go well, this could go sideways. I'm just accepting that that's the case and seeing if there's something that I can do to improve the outcome, but I don't have any control over it."

I think that's what it is: the uncertainty reminds us that we don't have control.

People don't want to be out of control.

They don't want to lose control.

They don't want to think that other people have control over them.

Okay, then escape. Escape from that anxiety.

There's freedom in escape. When you escape, you're throwing off the expectations and the beliefs that people have about you.

You're throwing off the chains and getting beyond those limitations by escaping, temporarily or permanently.

———

There is so much attention right now on being your own authentic self.

People are differentiating themselves in so many ways that people now call them snowflakes.

In the 12-step tradition, there's what they call terminal uniqueness, and that's where people get trapped. They get trapped in the idea that no one else understands them. No one has gone through what they've gone through.

If you stay away from those extremes and lean more toward the middle of living your authentic life, then the expectations, the limitations, or the naysayers don't bother you.

They don't trouble you because you know yourself better.

Furthermore, you're surrounding yourself with people who know you as you want to be known, and they're your cheerleaders, your champions.

They're your support network, they're the people who let you know that you're on the right track, or that maybe you should pay attention to something.

They are not criticizing you in a way that's belittling and dehumanizing. You want to live your life on your own terms, within the bounds of what is culturally expected.

We don't want people to be hounded down and killed, like my ex, who was being hunted by her family. That's what happens in some cultures when you step outside the cultural expectations. It's dangerous, so we have to be aware of the fact that there are consequences for doing this.

I have personally faced a lot of consequences.

In fact, I could probably write a whole book just about the outcomes of what happens when you step outside expectations, when you do escape. There are consequences for that.

You're not a child anymore. No one should be telling you what to do, forcing you to do anything. It's time to grow up, not just in terms of age. We have to mature.

Maturing emotionally and mentally means growing up.

I'll say it again. It's time to grow up. Don't hold yourself back from maturing.

I think some people are doing this these days, when they refer to maturing as 'adulting,' which is denigrating the whole idea of maturation.

They have to escape from this idea, this concept, that to be an adult means all these bad things, all the responsibility.

Take responsibility for your life.

It's so much better than just being at the whim of everyone else's expectations and limitations.

That is not good.

I'm an escape artist.

It's liberating and empowering to live like this. It's about living life on my own terms.

I'm bound by laws and rules, but I live free.

I know that people have expectations of me. However, I don't let their expectations of me limit how I live, what I do, and what I say.

When people find out that I've gone through a gender transition, they say things to me like, "Oh, you're so courageous. You're living your authentic self."

Sometimes I say back to them, with a smile, "Well, aren't you courageous? Aren't you living your authentic self?"

I think a lot of times, the look on their face tells me that they're not. They're not being brave in their own life. They're not living authentically.

It's about self-respect, so tell everyone who tries to limit you to F off.

It's also about self-worth and self-esteem.

If your self-worth and self-esteem aren't good, a sense of self isn't there. And to those who don't have a healthy sense of self, I want to say, "Why aren't you being as courageous as you want to be?"

Hey reader, my friend. This is for you, too.

Don't live vicariously through me.

You should be brave and live authentically.

Free.

If you want to live on your own terms, pursuing your own dreams, doing the kind of work you want to do in the world, spending your life with the kind of people you want to spend your life with, then you have to break free.

CHAPTER 2

DEFIANT

When it comes down to it, I am guided by my own moral compass. I'm grateful that my life experience has led me to the place where I am now.

And I trust that. I trust my own experiences.

After almost 58 years on this planet, I have learned many things. And I trust myself before I trust anyone else.

I have embraced my defiance.

To a certain degree, I would say my very birth was an act of defiance because they thought I was dead in the womb.

My mother told me that the doctor who treated my encephalitis told her my defiance set me apart from all the other children. And of the kids who got sick from the bad batch of MMR vaccine we had been given, I was the only one (there were about a dozen or so children who got very sick), who was able to rehab to the point of being able to walk independently, go back to school, and eventually become an athlete and serve in the military.

We shouldn't underestimate people. I have often been underestimated.

Too often, people think that children are exhibiting behaviors that are a nuisance or undesirable or should be punished out of them.

In an ideal world, people could find a way to hone in on the following statement:

"Oh, it looks like this kid might be naturally gifted with leadership energy. Let's teach them leadership skills. They might be somebody who's going to be standing in front of a group of people when they're talking because look how they command the living room. Look how they command the classroom. They take ownership of the space. They speak, and people listen. They tell jokes, they tell stories, they perform music."

Instead, I believe people think, "That kid's a troublemaker" or "Oh, how cute, that kid likes to be the class clown. How cute, that kid likes to perform in the living room for the family."

People are ignoring the potential of children too often. Especially if their behaviors are bumping up against cultural norms or social norms. Then we get labeled as defiant, hyperactive, or incorrigible. Possibly even sociopathic.

I think that's definitely what happened to me. I was underestimated and labeled a troublemaker.

But because of my default personality setting or post-encephalitis personality setting, which is probably more accurate, I didn't wait for other people to recognize potential in me. I went after my own potential.

Not only that, but I lifted myself up.

However, I know that many people, if not most, don't have that same drive.

Most people need the support and encouragement of others. They might need a little push from other people to do those things. I didn't need that. That's something I'm so grateful for.

The flip side of being a person who doesn't need to be coaxed, encouraged, or enticed to follow a particular career direction, or a particular direction in terms of how to integrate into society is that it meant I was doing it on my own for the most part.

I'll give my father credit for getting me involved in public speaking when I was ten. He did recognize my abilities, even though my school teachers didn't, and so many others didn't.

Even if I thought he was not paying attention, my father was doing the normal dad thing, thinking, "Let's get this kid into soccer."

"This kid is a chatterbox, let's put them up in front of an audience." I don't care what the motivation was.

My dad put me on a path starting at age ten, and I'm grateful for it now.

We spend so much time in school as children. And often parents don't get it, so if teachers and school counselors aren't recognizing these gifts, it can set people on a very different path.

I was very disruptive in school, belligerent, and argued with people.

I got into fights, I was bullied, and then I became a bully. (But of course, I was bullying the bullies, I didn't pick on the kids who were weaker or smaller than me.)

Defiant.

———

Being difficult in my childhood meant things like not dressing like a proper girl. That was one form of defiance.

Another would be that I was very talkative, not quite enough, and fidgety. That was a big thing that I would get in trouble for because I wouldn't stay in my seat. I would get up and walk around or fidget in my seat. I'd play with things at my desk and in church. For example, I'd be sitting in church next to my grandmother fidgeting, moving my feet, kicking my legs, and looking around.

I mean, come on, I was fascinated by all the

stained-glass. I was raised going to the Roman Catholic Church and there are so many beautiful buildings. There's stuff everywhere, including a dead guy hanging in the front.

My grandmother would hit me and say, "Sit still."

I wasn't dressing appropriately. I wasn't behaving correctly.

As a proper girl, I wasn't sitting in the right way.

———

I'm still difficult in many ways because I don't conform to ideological orthodoxies.

I can say that within the smaller community of trans people, I don't subscribe to a lot of what is considered to be the orthodoxy today, for example, that there's no such thing as biological or natal sex.

I don't think that way.

Instead, I believe in human biology and believe that I have a natal sex. It's based on my double X chromosomes and the fact that my body was made to produce large gametes (eggs). That could be enough, but of course, it's not.

There are plenty of other things that I don't agree with. I don't need to get into details about it. I don't think it is necessary.

Suffice it to say, I don't subscribe to orthodoxies. I don't care if they're social, political, or religious.

Not only that, but I'm not much of a joiner either. I rarely join a church, club, or team.

However, I am incredibly curious about things.

People have said, "Oh, you're a seeker."

I reply, "Well, I'm seeking knowledge. I'm seeking wisdom and ideas, but I'm not seeking a community to belong to."

I don't get my sense of belonging by joining things. I know belonging is important. And major corporations all around the world are adding the B for belonging to their DEI programs. As human beings, belonging to a tribe, clan, or family is very important.

However, for some reason, I don't get my sense of belonging from joining a group of people.

I have friends in all these different groups

from all walks of life and when I'm with them, that's when I feel a sense of belonging, either individually or in this very mixed group.

I'm very motivated by and attracted to other-ness.

People that are doing something other than the norm, other than expected intrigue me, because that's who I am.

Let's talk about the third space within the context of defiance.

The third space is for people who think dif-ferently or have questions or curiosity about things but don't automatically follow the script their family, religion, society, or cul-ture handed to them that says, "This is how you must behave. This is what you have to think, and this is what you should believe."

A lot of people don't subscribe to the cultural, social, religious, and familial scriptures. We're not conscripted into all of these things.

I think that the third space is where you can come to catch a breath and explore, investigate, learn, and question. It's okay to do all those things there.

You don't have some minister telling you, you can't question the orthodoxy of the religion.

You don't have some social justice warrior telling you you can't question the narrative your community is pushing on social media.

Furthermore, you can come to this third space, this safe space, as people call it. Or perhaps it's the brave space, whatever it is. It's this liminal space where you come together. It's coming together as individuals to test ideas and share them, to look for new ideas and concepts.

I read a book called 'The Cultural Creatives' about 20 years ago, when it came out, by Paul Ray and Sherry Ruth Anderson.

It was about a group of people called 'cultural creatives.' Very interesting. It's when people are in this space of being able to think, question, have curiosity, research, and investigate.

system for yourself, a value system. You can develop a new project that you want to work on. You can find people who have different perspectives from you. Then collaborate and bring together all of your ideas to create something amazing.

It can be a project, service, program, activity, or event. You don't get stuck in group think, where everyone just agrees with each other.

Rarely does someone want to be the one person in the group to say, "Yeah, I don't know if that'll work," or, "I don't really like that idea."

People are afraid to do that. People are scared of speaking out. Striking out on their own.

I think real defiance is voicing dissent, and this third space is the place where you can express disagreement without the typical negative consequences.

There may still be consequences stemming from which group of people you let come into the third space.

However, in the third space, there should be fairly minimal, if any, negative consequences for being a dissenter.

Change, whether in systems or society, typically comes when a dissenting voice is raised, and other people say, "Yeah, I agree with that."

When someone says, "You know what? We should be able to get married. Yes, we should be able to get married as gay and lesbian couples, that's right."

You're just dissenting from legal limitations. You say it out loud, and people say, "Yes, I agree with that."

Now how we get that done, that's where there are all kinds of disagreements.

The basic idea is if you want to make changes in your corporation, whether they be policy changes, programmatic changes, or whatever kind of changes you want to make, you're probably going to have to be a voice of dissent.

I don't think any corporation until more recently has said, "Let's get diversity and inclusion and equality or equity groups. Let's get a group together to start pointing out all the ways in which we're failing."

It was probably driven by employees, and ultimately by society that said, "These are things you should be paying attention to."

Those are the dissenters. And I think it's fascinating when the dissenters become the enforcers of the new norm.

Immediately, I think of the hippies, or now the boomers, who are the ones that have enforced a lot of BS on many people, but who were the dissenters.

They were rebelling against their parents, against the war, against social norms, and then they became the enforcers of a whole new set of norms that other generations are now pushing back on.

I understand that now people are calming down. They were dissenters when they were college students.

Then they become lawyers, bankers, medical doctors, and hospital administrators. They matured. I get it.

I've been a dissenter my whole life.

I'm still a dissenter, I'm still a defiant person.

We don't have to lose that as we age. I'm curious how so many of them lost it.

I wish there was a way to remind people who were dissenters, defiant, rebels about how they used to feel.

Where did they lose that and why?

Or has it just been buried?

System Limit

I have always avoided or limited my time in larger, more inflexible systems.

I served in the military, but not for a long period of time. I got in, and I got out.

I was also in law enforcement but for a short period. I got in, and I got out.

When you stay in a system, whether it's a particular corporation, government agency, or academia, you end up spending 20, 30, 40 years there.

That's how it used to be, but it is not as common anymore for most of the younger generations.

I think one of the benefits of moving around often, for me, is that I didn't get entrenched in a system. I didn't feel the pressure to go along with whatever the system was enforcing.

I probably wouldn't have been able to do that for very long. That's why I ended up leaving different systems because I just couldn't go along.

The consequences of this are that I don't have a pension, or a retirement account. Financial gains and losses are associated with this, which is really important because as we get older, we're going to need higher levels of healthcare.

That costs a lot of money, and it's not all covered by insurance or Medicare in our country. You have to foot some of the bill, so hopefully, I'm going to be okay.

But what's the alternative?

There's a tendency for human beings to want safety and security. These wishes are jeopardized by being defiant or rebellious because when you defy things you could lose your job.

You could lose your spouse, you could become

imprisoned, and you could lose your freedom.

Safety and security are very essential to most people. They're important to me, and I've been able to patch it together well enough to be where I am now, socially, physically, and financially.

But not everyone has the same skill set of how to patch things together, so that you don't have to rely on retiring or inheriting money from your family, which I will not.

The downside of going along to get along, as my dad used to say, is that you lose a sense of independence. Independence of thought, independence of action.

People who are truly invested in safety and security tend to be very invested in either doing the right thing according to different systems, or at least appearing like they're doing the right thing, which I think happens as well. People will behave in certain ways because it's what's expected of them, from their family, job, church, culture, ethnicity, racial group, and whatever identity they have. They're not really stretching. They're not exploring. They're not learning about new ideas and new activities.

If a person is staying in a system by their own conscious choice, that's fine. But I bet most people are trapped in systems. They're trapped in the expectations of their sex, occupation, role in the family, and place in the community.

They've trapped themselves.

Wanting to be ourselves, wanting to be who we are exactly as we are, as long as we don't interfere with other people's ability to be who they are, and we're not breaking any laws, is going to be limited if we are tethering ourselves to an inflexible system.

The 700 Club

I remember when I was a teenager, I would watch the '700 Club,' a television program that had Christian evangelical preachers on it.

My friends would ask me, "Why do you watch that?"

I used to say, "I want to know what they're thinking."

As a teenager, I would take in information

from a very large cross-section of people, and look at many different organizations, and what they were doing.

Not only that, but I subscribed to various kinds of magazines.

Even now, every couple of years, I get a new magazine subscription because I want to learn new things.

For example, I just subscribed to 'Skeptic' magazine.

People have probably called me skeptical, so maybe I'm one. So I want to read what skeptics are writing about.

I also get 'Vegetarian News.' And I'm not a vegetarian.

I read all different types of blogs, books, and magazines because I want to know a lot of things from a lot of places from a lot of different peoples' perspectives.

I don't like just being around people who say what I say, think what I think, and agree with me. That's not interesting to me. I find that boring.

Because I'm constantly engaging and taking in new information, information that either aligns or doesn't with what I'm currently thinking about something, it gives me the opportunity to stop and think, "Oh, okay, so this is a new piece of information. I'm going to check it out."

Am I going to accept it? If I accept it, does it replace something, or can I just weave it into my own thoughts on that topic? Am I going to outright reject it?

Am I going to reject the entire thing, or just pieces of it? Why am I doing that? Am I having a visceral reaction to it?

Or maybe I don't understand it. If I don't, then I'm going to go seek out someone who has a better understanding. Perhaps the author of the article I'm reading, or someone who works at the organization that's championing something in the world.

If I don't understand it, I'll look in the dictionary for words I don't comprehend. I'll also talk to people about a concept that I don't understand.

If I've never heard about it, or if it's using words that I'm unfamiliar with, then I'm not going to reject it until I know more about it. In some ways, that's me being defiant.

That's a form of defiance because I'm not automatically accepting it or rejecting it. I'm curious about it, and I'm considering it.

I don't watch FOX, MSNBC, or CNN. When I watch the news, I like to watch C-SPAN. I want to see the camera focused right on the politicians as they're talking in the congressional chambers.

I want to hear directly from them, I don't want the minister telling me what God wants.

Likewise, I don't want the newscasters telling me what the politician said.

I'm going to listen straight to the politician.

I listen to people, not to others telling me about people.

I listen to what people tell me.

When I say to people, "I don't watch the news, but I watch C-SPAN sometimes."

Most people say, "What is C-SPAN?"

They don't even know that we have this channel that is practically on 24/7 in Washington, D.C.

My reply is, "Well, that's where you can actually listen to what's happening every day in congressional committee meetings, or hearings."

No Replicas

I surround myself with people who have very different experiences in the world than me and have distinct ideas about things than I do.

I'm friends with people that others can't stand to be around. I really enjoy their company.

They're a little rough around the edges, but I don't mind because I enjoy their perspectives. I don't share them most of the time, but I enjoy being around people who can formulate their own thoughts and opinions about things, when they're well-researched in their own right.

I don't have to agree with them. I'm not just consuming information from videos, books, news articles, and television, but also directly from people who are in my friendship circle.

I also don't interact with many people who are primarily strangers to me.

However, I'm involved in online networks, both clinical and more social, where there are definitely people that either don't accept, condone, or don't approve of what I've done (transition). But otherwise, they're very lovely people.

It challenges me to make sure that I'm staying honest, maintaining integrity, not going off into some emotional plea for acceptance, and remaining more rational in my dealings with others.

When I want to interact with other people, I have to be conscientious of the other person. I don't know their experience, and they don't know mine, but we're going to interact with each other.

If I expect them to think how I think, act how I act, to have the same experience that I've had, I'm obviously going to be sorely mistaken.

As far as I know, there is no replica of me.

I don't think I've been cloned.

If I want to be on friendly terms with other human beings, I have to be willing to acknowledge and accept that they have viewpoints that I may disagree with or beliefs I don't believe in.

That's what their life experience, culture, religion, whatever it is, has led them to believe.

They could be medical doctors, or biologists, saying, "I'm a biologist. I can't deny that there's such a thing as natal sex that exists in animals, including humans and plants."

When I interact with trans people who say they can't be around someone who "denies their existence," they're really limiting themselves.

They're unable to regulate their own emotions and tolerate that distress enough to be able to hear a person's perspective.

I do allyship training all the time. One of the components of allyship that some people stress a lot more than I do is the idea that if someone's offended by what you've said, you need to respond.

I'd say just listen to what they're telling you. We don't do the reverse.

We don't tell the offended person, "Well, are you listening to them?"

We don't hold the offended person as accountable as "the offender."

I think that that's important because it's similar to bullying. We can't just go right to the bully and say 'It's all about you'.

We don't tend to look at all the players in the struggle, so to speak.

We're only looking at one side of it.

Visceral Reflection

I think it's helpful to be able to take an inventory of the beliefs, ideas, concepts, and values that we hold. Typically, we don't know we hold certain values until an event occurs, and then we have a strong reaction, either for it or against it.

That's when we learn, "Oh, this is something I value. This is something that I have a strong belief about."

When that moment arises, we can make a mental note of it or write it down, as I do with everything, and then revisit it at a later date.

What event happened, and what did it trigger?

What kind of visceral, a visceral yes, or a visceral no did I experience? And why?

Learn about the self, and be reflective and retrospective.

Take the time to understand yourself better.

The better we can understand ourselves, the better we'll be able to understand others.

The more empathetic we can be with ourselves, the more empathetic we can be toward others.

The more self-compassion we have, the more compassionate we can be toward others.

And the more honest we are with ourselves, the more honest we can be with other people.

It starts with the self.

When I was 14 years old, I said to a friend of mine, "I really hate Chris,"

She was another girl who was in the all-girls school I attended.

She asked me, "Why do you hate Chris?"

I said, "Because she's so sarcastic."

She looked at me, and I said, "What?"

She replied, "You're the most sarcastic person I know."

To which I replied, "I am?"

I didn't realize I was a sarcastic person.

That's the first time I remember really being face-to-face with that mirror. That happens when you see someone who is so much like you, and you hate them for it.

It happens a lot with kids toward their parents. All of a sudden, as you get older, you start taking on more and more of your parents' attributes, which you rebelled against when you were in your teens and 20s.

In some cultures and social settings, it is an act of defiance to be self-reflective. In some settings, we're not allowed to, and we're not encouraged to march to the beat of our own drum.

For example, when I was a kid in Catholic school learning the catechism, I'd get smacked if I asked questions that the nuns didn't like.

There was no encouragement of curiosity. It was just, "No. Wrong question. Bad child." Thankfully, whatever kind of message they were trying to convey didn't stop me. But unfortunately, such actions stop a lot of people.

It happens in the more orthodox religious communities and cultural communities. It's like a pressure cooker. Everyone is around you all the time, reinforcing the norms and reminding you of the taboos.

Part of self-reflection is to say, "Well, do I agree with those norms?"

Defiant people are more likely to challenge the status quo.

It is important to know yourself and what you stand for.

It's important to know why you stand for it and how to articulate what it is you believe, what you think, and what you want.

Doing this is going to help you navigate life, and figure out not just what occupation you want to work in, but also which employers you want to work for.

It's going to help you know what kind of mate you want to end up with and have a family with, whatever that means for you.

Do you want to live in the country? Do you want to live in the suburbs? Perhaps you want to live in the inner city? Do you want to live in the United States?

It helps you orient yourself to everything. If you're a person of faith, what does that mean? Are you going to join a church, or are you going to just go around visiting different places of worship?

It's a helpful compass. People who just go along to get along, and I hear of this all the time when I'm doing coaching, have ended up in marriages, occupations, or careers for 10, 15, 20, 30 years, and then reflect on it and say, "What have I done? What have I done with my life?"

They felt like they were being led through a path, and they didn't question it. When they did, they didn't like the consequences, so they just shut their mouth and kept doing it.

All along, it wasn't what they wanted to do. I think people are well-intentioned, but those intentions don't matter if it's steering someone down the wrong course. That's a form of defiance because you're just starting your own path.

Suppose a person is so highly sensitive to people being unhappy and unfriendly toward them. In that case, they might want to become more defiant to have people be friendlier to them and experience less conflict in their lives.

Then they'll never be without conflict entirely, but the more defiant you are, the more friction you're going to have in your life. The more skillful you become at managing and mitigating conflict, the more of it you can deal with.

That's been my path.

In life, I've become more defiant, so to speak, or I have remained defiant.

But all the while, I've developed skills, including getting a master's degree in Conflict Analysis and Resolution, to be able to mitigate, manage, transform, and transcend conflict.

It's probably one of the most important things I've been able to do, learning conflict management skills.

I think it's true that people who are the most successful in the most significant ways possible, meaning inventors and people who have done great things in the world, have defied expectations, beat the odds, and crafted their own path.

We should be more like them.

Defiantly.

TRUSTING

Being suspicious, untrusting, and keeping people at a distance is not a very fulfilling way to live. It limits our access to joy, vitality, excitement, and mystery.

When we distrust, we don't open ourselves up to other people. And if we don't open ourselves up to other people, then we don't open ourselves up to different opportunities that may come our way.

I understand why some people are not trusting. They may have experienced someone getting in their way and betraying their trust in the past. There are malicious people out there, or at least people who do malicious things.

I understand why people would be interested in being very protective of themselves. I don't want to give the impression that I think people who do that are silly. There's a purpose for it. In the short term, it's a reaction or a response to a betrayal of some sort.

However, you still have to figure out how to move on and not project that distrust onto every person you meet, which is what happens if people don't process it.

Around the year 2000, I read a book called 'Vietnam: Lotus in a Sea of Fire' by Thích Nhâ't Hanh. He's a Vietnamese Buddhist monk who created this system of Buddhism called Engaged Buddhism, where you walk around instead of sitting lotus-style while meditating in the mountains or forests.

He had this passage in his book where he said people withhold information because they don't trust how others will respond and because of their inability to navigate potentially upsetting news.

He proposed some questions that can be asked when people lie to you: Why is that person lying to me? The second part is, what about me is contributing to their need to lie to me?

Think of children. Why do children lie to their parents? It's because they're afraid of being punished.

You ask them, "Did you eat the cookie?"

They say no, even though it's all over their mouth because they don't want to be reprimanded.

As adults, we do the same. We withhold information, or we outright deceive people. We embellish the truth because something about the other person, maybe either in our personal experience with them or in our assumption of them, makes us feel and think that we are going to be punished for it.

For a lot of people, the ability to extend trust to others can be impacted by the environment in which they grew up.

For example, children who grow up in environments with a lot of deceit and secrecy will carry that part of themselves into adulthood.

So, if you grow up in a home with addiction, there's always secrecy around that.

If there's some sort of abuse and neglect in the family, there's often secrecy.

When you keep secrets, and the children are involved in the secret-keeping, they learn not to trust.

———————

At 14 years old, I thought I was all grown up.

I had a certain level of street smarts, so to speak because I was a pretty rough-and-tumble kind of kid.

I had some kinds of intelligence, but I didn't have others. For example, I had book smarts and knew how to keep myself out of trouble.

But I didn't have emotional intelligence, which is something that's not innate. It has to be modeled, it has to be demonstrated. It has to be cultivated. What's more, we typically get skills like that from the adults in our life.

So here I was, in this group home for delinquents. There were six to eight of us in the home, and we had one 'houseparent' who would stay overnight with us. During the day, we were at our school campus outside the home.

My houseparent recognized that I didn't have

very much emotional maturity. I didn't know how to regulate my emotions, tolerate distress, and communicate my needs effectively.

I didn't know how to navigate through all the inevitable uncertainties in life, and how to mitigate the constant conflict I was encountering and generating.

I was both mature and immature at the same time. I was trusting to a certain degree.

However, thankfully, since adolescence, or perhaps a little bit younger, I have been very attentive to my own signals. So if I get a signal from the limbic part of my brain that says, "Danger, danger," I walk away.

I've had extreme encounters that would have dramatically altered the course of my life because of some bad, predatory people. But I was so fortunate to have that sort of 6th sense.

Trust Yourself

We have to learn how to trust ourselves and our instincts.

At the basic level, this should have started when we were infants, and we had adults in our lives who responded to our cries. People who have learned to trust from childhood will not have as much trouble trusting throughout their lives, and they will even be able to rebound from betrayal more easily.

On the other hand, people who grew up with a lack of attachment and a lack of trust will have to figure out how to trust themselves and others.

A person who was raised in an environment where a narcissistic parent perpetually gaslighted them means that they aren't able to know how to trust their own instincts. They were constantly being overridden by their emotionally immature parents trying to make everything about them.

That kind of person is going to need a support network. They're going to need someone or a small group of people to whom they can say, "This is what I'm hearing, this is what I'm seeing, and this is what I'm experiencing. What do you think it is?"

Initially, they have to learn how to trust their own instincts by learning how to pay attention to what their instincts are telling them.

You lose your ability to trust those instincts when you grow up in an environment where all of your natural instincts are denied, suppressed, repressed, ridiculed, or demeaned.

I learned this a long time ago, probably in the 1980s. Someone gave me a book that said that the way to start trusting your own instincts is to start with the autonomic ones.

For example, if you feel hungry, eat. Don't put off eating.

If you feel like you need to go to the bathroom, don't hold it. Go to the bathroom.

Start noticing and responding to your basic instinct signals that are coming from your body.

When you feel sleepy, go to sleep. Take a nap, go to bed.

You start to learn to trust your own instincts once you begin learning, paying attention, and responding to your signals. From there, you can expand it more and more.

Too many people are just ignoring their own signals, "Oh, I'll sleep later, or I don't want to get up to get some water right now. I'll just hold my pee, the bladder will take a hit for a while."

That's not only terrible as you become older and start having problems, but it's also awful to override your systems.

But how will we ever be able to establish trust in our instincts about other people if we can't even pay attention to our own bodily instincts or urges, the things that keep us alive and healthy, like eating, staying hydrated, and sleeping?

The way to trust the self is to listen. Listen to the signals the body is sending , the thoughts that are coming, and the emerging feelings.

However, we still need to decipher which thoughts and feelings to act on.

We might be feeling hungry, but are we over-eating? We might be getting hunger signals, but we've already eaten. Maybe we're just gorging ourselves.

We have to distinguish whether it's a healthy or an unhealthy signal.

Trust yourself.

Trust Your Environment

We need to live in a space where we can trust that we're safe.

Being able to trust the environment you're in requires self-inquiry, "Am I in a safe space?" Because sometimes you can be in a place with no one else but yourself, and still not feel safe.

And why don't you feel safe? Either you don't trust that the environment is safe, or you don't trust that you can handle it if it's not.

We're talking about our homes, workplaces, friends' homes, the streets we walk down, and the restaurants and the movie theaters we go to.

There's a certain level of agency that we have, and there's a certain level that we don't have. We can't control everything and everyone.

As a trans man in Florida, I feel perfectly safe. However, I'm not stupid. I know that something random could happen, but I'm not going to focus my energy on that.

There's a saying that goes, "What we resist, persists," but what we focus on influences what we think is going to happen. We're creating the scenario in our own minds.

Then, we feel stress and a strain on our bodies when we are in a state of emergency. We're going to be stressing our muscles. Then that tension is going to constrict our blood vessels, and that's going to restrict blood flow, which limits the available oxygen. That's not going to be good for us physiologically. It's probably going to disrupt our sleep. And when our sleep is disturbed, our circadian rhythm is dysregulated, and all the other systems in our body will follow suit. It's harmful to our physical well-being.

It's also bad for our emotional and mental well-being because we're putting a lot of stress on our thinking. We're so hyper-focused on what could happen. Nothing has really happened, so we're either feeling anxious or depressed about some potential fear.

Maybe we're trying to numb those concerns with substances, sex, shopping, porn, or video games. We're distracting ourselves to the point that we're not really engaging with others. As a result, our relationships are going to suffer. Our emotions are on high alert and messing with our thoughts.

Some people are going to completely withdraw from their friend networks and relationships and then isolate themselves.

Don't do that! Trust your environment, and/or seek out an environment you trust.

Trusting Others

When we were kids, we only interacted with a smaller group of people. As we get older, we're exposed to a larger group of people.

We learn more about trust in adolescence because that's when we start to explore our environment and the people we interact with.

In our adolescence, we were probably at different levels of exposure, and we need to trust and hope that our trust is with a safe person.

We need to be simultaneously paying attention to the signals we're getting from all these other people and how it makes us feel, while also not creating any unnecessary distance between us and them.

There's a scale to it. We trust people a little

bit, and then we trust them a little more. It comes in waves. And unless something severe happens, we just keep going. There could be little bumps, stops, and starts, but nothing so significant as to veer us off in a different direction.

And so we develop trust slowly over time, in our childhood, adolescence, and maybe even young adulthood, as we start to go out into the world more and experience various environments and interact with a much larger group of people.

I'm a believer in giving someone the benefit of the doubt.

Just because a person has done something to another person that violated their trust, that doesn't mean they're going to do the same thing to me.

We do treat people differently. I don't prejudge people based on what other people say. I've been prejudged my entire life, so I'm very cautious and weary about taking on other people's judgments. I will take them into consideration and keep them in the back of my mind, but I'm not going to let them dictate me.

I know what it feels like when someone says, "Oh, you can't trust Zander," or "Zander is a bad person," or "Zander has wrong thoughts."

People go, "Oh, okay," and they never connect with me.

They never actually try to get to know me.

I don't want to be the kind of person who does that to other people.

I was a social worker at the Health Care for Homeless Veterans program, and I was one of the few social workers who would work with the veterans who were on the sex offender registry.

We couldn't put them into any of our housing because people on the sex offender registry aren't eligible for federal housing.

However, they could come in, shower, and wash and dry their clothes. They could meet with me, and I could give them some food and beverages, as well as new clothes to take with them.

While there were a lot of things I could do for them, there were also a lot of restrictions.

I chose to help because they're still human beings. They're homeless, they need to clean up, and they need to eat. Another kind of veteran that would come in was the angry veteran who would scream and curse.

I was one of the few social workers who would work with them. Perhaps it was because I was the only man on the team. The women were usually too afraid of them.

But even if I hadn't transitioned, I still wouldn't have been scared of them.

If someone is angry, I'm going to conclude that it's most likely justifiable. I'd be furious if I fought in a war, and now I live on the streets. It's a combination of factors that leads to that point. But now they're here with me.

Many people, the police, for example, wouldn't even let them into the clinic. When that happened, I would go outside and bring them into my office.

The police would tell me to keep my office door open, but I wouldn't, because they deserve respect. They also deserve privacy and confidentiality. As a result, the police would stand outside the door.

I trusted myself to have enough rapport with them so they could get the message, "Hey man, I'm treating you like a human being. My hope is you're going to treat me the same way."

Inevitably, they started coming on Fridays when I was the triage person for the homeless program .

I had to trust them, but I also had to trust myself. I had to trust the other people around me, including a big government system and the police.

I had to believe that if something went haywire, and I was unable to get myself out of a problem, the police officer right outside my door was going to come right in.

It's a multi-layer of trust.

However, if I didn't trust myself to get out of it, then I probably wouldn't meet with them in my office.

If I did, it would be with the door open and the police standing there, but they probably wouldn't trust me. They probably wouldn't want to meet with me.

I had to figure out a way to meet their needs, my needs, and the needs of the agency simultaneously.

So, who do you trust?

Trusting Systems

The last thing is trusting our institutions and systems.

What I've experienced over the course of my lifetime is that it might take a while to get there, but most of the time, the right thing happens.

People in the United States worked tirelessly for same-sex marriage for four decades. It finally happened!

Things like gay and lesbian people being able to serve in the military and able to adopt children have all been codified into law.

There was no guarantee that we were ever going to get those rights because of certain politicians who were against same-sex marriage, but the tide eventually turned.

Some people seem to find themselves being sent to prison for things that they haven't done. And so, thankfully, we have all these wonderful systems and networks that are parallel to the criminal justice system.

For example, some non-profit organizations

read through all the case law and all the trial transcripts. They find ways to retry the case, and innocent people are set free.

Trump's presidency garnered polarizing opinions, but one good thing from his administration was when he granted freedom to hundreds of people who had committed nonviolent crimes, most of whom were black people.

There's also the trust in religion. If someone is a person of faith, and they have experienced something that breaks their trust in that faith, that doesn't mean they have to become an atheist. The pendulum swings from believer to non-believer, from theist to atheist.

And in the middle of the road, there is maybe just non-theist, which is the word that Dalai Lama and people like me use to describe ourselves. I'm not a believer or a disbeliever.

I just shrug and say, "Huh, interesting."

It's slightly different from agnostic, and it just means that I'm curious and open to looking into other philosophies and faith systems.

I get that people give up on religion. They've been harmed, abused, and hurt. They feel betrayed. However, they could focus narrowly and keep their feelings of betrayal focused on the offender instead of the whole religious organization. Find another place, a new church, in the system. Instead of completely giving up on it, you have to figure out where you want to go.

So, believe it or not, I actually have some pretty good trust in certain systems.

Take another look at the systems you interact with, and see where you can put your trust.

It's not always going to be true for everyone, but if you want to live an extraordinary life, you have to be willing to take extraordinary risks.

One of those is that you need to take the risk of trusting.

Trust has allowed me to go places, experience things I probably never would have experienced, and meet people I probably would have never met.

If I were to be a person looking at myself at

the age of 10, 15, or 20, there's no way I could have ever predicted the life that I'm living now. It's beyond comprehension.

It's because I trust myself first and foremost. I'm a nonconformist and a risk-taker. I trust people. I take risks, and they pay off.

My friends say I have the Midas touch. I applied to one college and got in. I applied to one graduate school, one seminary, and one social work program. I got every job I ever applied for.

Part of it is that I don't just apply to any random job. I do my research. I want to know what that company is all about, what they do, what their products are, what their services are, what their mission is, how long they've been in business, and who runs the business. I want to know what kind of message they're putting out to the world. That lets me know if I'd like to work there.

We have to do some due diligence. We can't just step out into the middle of the street with oncoming traffic and hope they're going to stop or swerve.

We have to be smart about it. We have to stand at the curb, look both ways like we were taught in kindergarten, and then cross the street.

We need to be smart about the risks we take, but that doesn't mean we shouldn't take them.

Do you want to carve your own path?

Are you sick and tired of doing what everyone else is doing or telling you to do?

Do you feel constrained in having to do what everyone else is doing because that's what people applaud?

Then chart out your own course.

Playing it safe might keep us alive, but it doesn't give us the opportunity to thrive.

Trust me.

INDEPENDENT

In the face of what we clinically call 'traumatic events,' we often seek the elusive quality of 'resilience.'

We try to instill this virtue in individuals by saying things like, "People are resilient" or "Children are resilient."

These are commonly uttered phrases, although not everyone fully understands what 'resilience' really means.

Imagine, if you will, the image of a phoenix rising from the ashes. It serves as an apt depiction of the process. It visualizes the sequence of encountering something, going through it, processing it, and then rising again.

This ethereal ascension signifies a return to our former selves before the incident, trauma, or challenge.

However, a similar concept of anti-fragility, or even better, post-traumatic growth, in clinical terms, goes beyond mere rebound or resilience.

"What are you talking about, Zander?"

Ok, let me dive in. Post-traumatic growth involves not just bouncing back, but actually growing from adversity. Think of Hydra, the serpentine creature of Greek mythology, that grows back two heads after one is severed.

The difference is that challenges empower us to build a form of strength similar to the physiological response of our bones and skeletal system when subjected to tension.

Our bones become stronger when we run or jump. Similarly, our mental and emotional well-being can be strengthened by adversity, thereby improving our overall mental and emotional well-being.

These days, there seems to be an overwhelming abundance of adversity, challenges, and obstacles that people face regularly.

It's so daunting and difficult that there seems to be no way out. It's as if people have imagined themselves trapped in a perpetual state of oppression or limitation.

Our response to those feelings brings me back to a lot of the influences I had growing up, with Buddhism and Taoism, especially the Buddhist teachings that emphasized three approaches: hiding from something, rushing recklessly toward it, or opening your eyes, paying attention, and determining the best course of action.

It was about finding the balance between attachment and detachment, a state of non-attachment.

I have non-attachment to these traumas, so that I can grow from them.

This is similar to anti-fragility or independence. There are many words to describe this approach to life.

It doesn't mean that you're always impervious to the reality of what's going on around you. It doesn't mean you're not affected. It's just that these traumas won't destroy your mind.

There are all kinds of things going on around me, and to be honest, it would send some people into a tailspin of anxiety.

But personally, I don't have anxiety or depression. I deal with these situations by putting them in their proper context.

For example, I am currently facing a challenge with far-reaching implications for my livelihood and reputation. It's just one thing happening in my personal universe, so to speak.

However, my approach is to adopt a 'wait and see' attitude. I recognize my extensive track record of credibility and excellence in my work.

I know that from time to time, I'm going to run into someone who takes great offense to what I say or how I say it, and that's inevitable.

I have a contract with a client who seems to think that one complaint out of thousands of people I've worked with over the course of two and a half years carries enough weight that I could lose my contract.

So I have to strike a balance. I cannot dismiss

the concern outright as something trivial, nor can I allow it to drag me into a state of despair, panic, or crisis response.

I have to navigate this situation while maintaining balance.

And you need to work to have independence of thought and knowledge to some extent, so that you can overcome challenges.

There's a Stoic saying, "The obstacle is the way," that Ryan Holiday writes about a lot. It means that you don't see obstacles as barriers, but as opportunities to learn and grow.

Stoicism doesn't get much praise in our society, however, and is often associated with coldness, calculation, and detachment. But that's a misconception.

Stoicism doesn't advocate being cold and detached. In fact, a person who is cold and detached is not being stoic. They're probably just being rigid in their thinking.

With anti-fragility, you cannot be rigid. It's about finding the right balance.

As my father used to say, if you are too flexible, your brain can fall out of your head. You can't be so open that your brain falls out, but you also can't be so rigid or closed-off.

If you're not flexible, every encounter and person becomes a constant "trigger", as some people say.

However, if you embrace being anti-fragile, you can be in the company of people who say things you don't particularly like or agree with. You can be in the company of people who believe things you don't. Even if you absolutely loathe what they've done or what they think, it doesn't shake you to your core. Why should it?

After all, you didn't participate in those same actions. Why should you be so invested in being angry about it?

It becomes about the issue rather than the individual.

This perspective is consistent with a negotiation tactic I learned in college, which is to separate people from problems. If you can separate people from problems, it opens up a whole world of possibilities for this ability to have an anti-fragile frame of reference.

People often describe themselves as codependent when the emotions of others heavily influence their emotional well-being.

On the other hand, some individuals proclaim their independence and use it as the antithesis of codependency.

A third option that exists is interdependence, which falls between codependency and interdependence. If we think of independence as being lonely or isolated, and codependence as emotional enmeshment, interdependence offers a middle ground.

In our culture, especially in the United States, independence is typically associated with being a lone wolf, having few people around you. Interdependence allows us to cultivate a balanced approach. It means having our own thoughts, feelings, reactions, and decision-making skills, while also being considerate of others.

For example, in my marriage, I can't ignore my wife's feelings and needs, but I also won't base my entire life solely on what she wants.

That would be codependent.

Instead, interdependence requires negotiation. This negotiation extends to all aspects of life, including jobs, friendships, and organizations in which I participate.

It's a constant negotiation for interdependence with other people who have their own thoughts, feelings, experiences, wants, and needs.

An independent person must become comfortable with the idea of being disliked by others, because independent thinkers and doers are unlikely to conform just to maintain harmony.

It takes a special kind of courage to take a stand that may not be popular. So you have to be comfortable with being disliked, and you have to be comfortable with a certain amount of disapproval.

However, being independent also frees you from expectations and conformity. Another way to describe it is nonconformity or counterculturalism.

Personally, my nonconformity and counter-cultural mindset empowers me. It gives me tenacity, confidence, and the energy to believe (and I'm open to feedback) that I'm mostly on a righteous path, doing good work, and I trust that.

I have to be able to be open to feedback, and I have to be able to tolerate the criticism that comes.

As a person of independent thought, action, and feeling, I can't expect to never face criticism. I have to be able to withstand the distress that comes from people passionately disagreeing with me, even if they are screaming, yelling, and saying some pretty harsh things.

That's just the way it is.

If you're going to go out on your own, you have to be at least prepared to hear people say, "You're crazy," "You're wrong," or "You're creating more problems."

It comes with the territory.

The techniques I first learned to withstand this kind of negative energy are grounding techniques. One of them is called 'meshing.'

It involves visualizing a piece of mesh or cheesecloth running straight down the center of your body, from your head, neck, chest, and torso, both legs and through your ankles.

This imagery allows all the negativity, energy, and words directed at you to simply pass through, as if you've transformed yourself into the mesh.

Another technique is anchoring. There are different ways of doing this, but one I find effective is to visualize a ship's anchor dropping from the bottom of your spine and going into the earth or the bottom of the ocean.

You can just imagine that you're on a boat. It keeps you tied down so you don't drift too far and allows you to weather the storms.

We can use a similar mental approach to emotionally withstand the negativity and strong energy directed at us because of something we have said or not said, or something we have done or not done.

In life, we never know when we might upset someone. For some people, it feels like walking through an active minefield, not knowing where you might step on an explosive topic.

I can certainly relate to this feeling in my own life over the past few years. I have come to realize that avoiding the minefield is not an option.

I'm not going around the minefield. I'm going through it. But I'm not just going to walk through it, because if I step on a cultural bomb, I'm just going to get blown up.

I have to figure out how to navigate through this field of invisible mines without accidentally setting one off.

This minefield is filled with various peer pressures. Individuals are compelled to conform to group norms by cultural, familial, religious, and social pressures. Deviating from these norms, whether minimally or significantly, has consequences that some people don't want to endure, so they don't deviate.

However, some individuals abandon all concern for their well-being and run recklessly across the field, never making it to the other side.

Navigating this challenging terrain involves

facing numerous obstacles and pressures, whether at work, home, or school.

The significance of these pressures intensified around 2015, especially during the Clinton-Trump election year in the United States. It caused a lot of stress, and people started to react in various peculiar ways.

I know people who bought gas masks, thinking they would be taken to internment camps. These were licensed mental health professionals who then passed all that stress and anxiety on to their clients.

Hm. That's not good.

Unbroken

From a clinical perspective, brokenness may not be an official concept, but it underlies the work of trauma or trauma-informed therapists. Some people have experienced difficulties so severe that they may have broken their spirit, will, or desire to live.

Acknowledging the challenges we face is crucial, and certain situations can indeed knock us off our feet, like a strong gust of wind. It's just going to happen from time to time. These circumstances can range from someone punching you in the face to being sexually assaulted. These are situations that can really knock someone off balance.

However, I disagree with giving people permission to stay broken.

I believe it takes away people's ability to heal from their brokenness or from the pain of what was broken. Instead of holding out hope for them and supporting the gradual development of their own hope, we tend to let them off the hook.

And we say, "Well, they can't do better, or they can't do more because they have all these obstacles, all these challenges."

To me, however, this is robbing them of their ability to persevere, to achieve, and to find their own version of succeeding.

It's not about forcing my way on them. It's about empowering them to find their own way. The language used may not explicitly say that people should stay broken, but that's essentially what's happening.

For two years, from age 17 to 19, I was in a relationship with an older woman. She was in her mid-20s, and she had lived so much more life than I had.

She had served in the military, traveled abroad, and been in relationships. It was a very different dynamic than my 17-year-old experience.

It turned out that she had problems with alcohol, and I hadn't grown up around drug abuse or alcoholism. I felt completely disoriented in this situation, and my world began destabilizing.

Society had led me to believe that women were safer than men, but this relationship proved otherwise. I was supposed to feel safe, but I didn't. In the mid-1980s, there weren't many support services for gay and lesbian people experiencing interpersonal violence.

Where does a young girl go when her abuser is a woman? Where do I go for help?

I tried to reach out to shelters or local resources, but they didn't take people like me. A lesbian.

I called the police, but that didn't help. They made an anti-gay remark, and that was the end of it.

I desperately searched for a way out of this ordeal, but I was confused. I was so overwhelmed that I turned to drinking as an escape and a way to numb myself. I developed a problem with drinking, although it was short-lived.

Eventually, I found the courage to confide in my father, who rescued me from the abuse. Still, I was completely heartbroken and utterly lost. I didn't really understand what had happened to me.

I went to live with an aunt, but I hid in the house out of fear that she would find me if I ventured outside.

My life took a dark turn when I started hanging out with people who used heavy drugs. I was just petrified to live my life, and even I tried to kill myself twice.

Then I joined the military to avoid worrying about leaving the house, staying alive, and doing drugs. I joined the Coast Guard in 1988.

I got out of the destructive cycle, but to be honest, I never stopped looking over my shoulder and wondering when she was going to come back into my life and ruin it until 2023.

During those two years together, I watched

her make phone calls to get her ex-girlfriends fired from their jobs. I kept waiting for her to come after me in a similar way. Though she never did, the fear persisted.

I finally tracked her down and confronted her, which was the turning point. Over the years, the fear began to diminish, but it wasn't until I confronted her that I really let go of the emotional burden. And I haven't really thought about it since. I have no emotional reaction whatsoever when I tell this story.

None at all. I could go into detail about all the physical, mental, emotional, and sexual abuse. And I have, several times, but it no longer brings up feelings for me.

I had to face the obstacle head on to release its hold on me. I thought, 'The obstacle is the way.' That was the lesson I learned.

The unbroken aspect of the relationship came when I finally accepted that I was not to blame for the abuse.

I realized that she was the abusive one and that I had every right to leave.

When my father rescued me, I felt bad about leaving because I knew she was in a dire financial situation. I knew it would be difficult for her without my income at that time. Even with all the bullshit she put me through, I was concerned for her well-being.

Once I understood that I wasn't to blame, I took charge of my life. Although the proverbial bones had healed, there was still weakness in the broken places.

There was still a tendency for them to break again in the same place where they had been broken before.

When I finally contacted her, via email, I didn't confront her directly. I just expressed my feelings and moved on. In that moment, it felt like the healing process had become much stronger.

This is similar to Kintsugi, a Japanese art form in which broken pottery is repaired with gold, making it even stronger in the broken places. We often use this metaphor in post-traumatic growth.

Another perspective is that the cracks in life are where the light comes through.

Despite the pain of brokenness, there are ways to see it as a source of growth and positive change.

Un-oblivious

Not being oblivious means not walking around like an ostrich with your head in the sand. It means paying attention and being aware. It means not ignoring important signals and cues from our environment.

Our limbic system is designed to keep us safe by alerting us to potential dangers. For example, some people claim that we are facing a 'trans genocide.'

They throw this term around so casually. They really believe that a genocide is happening or coming, and so they're constantly in 'Danger! Danger! Danger!' limbic system response mode.

If you live like that, you won't be able to pay attention. You're going to be oblivious to all the real signs and signals of the things you really need to pay attention to.

We can also be oblivious because we're intoxicated.

Intoxication, whether from substances, obsessions, or excessive behaviors, can also cloud our awareness.

When we are intoxicated, our brains release

pleasure chemicals that can distract us from real issues and make us absent minded to important matters.

After challenging experiences like these, our natural response may be to become hyper-vigilant or defensive. However, striking a balance between forgetfulness and hypervigilance is crucial.

It involves acknowledging past difficulties, ensuring that we remove harmful influences from our lives, and adopting a state of attentive awareness without constant fear.

In difficult situations or relationships, our natural response is to be on high alert, ready to defend ourselves.

It's like a pendulum swinging between heightened awareness and going on the offensive. This hypervigilance, especially for people with post-traumatic stress, is the opposite of obliviousness.

We don't want to be oblivious, but we also don't want to be overly vigilant.

The balance is between awareness and vigilance.

Yes, terrible things have happened, but they are in the past. Hopefully, that person or those people are no longer in your life.

And if they are, you have to figure out how to distance yourself from them and possibly lose contact with them.

One of the biggest challenges for therapists working with people in abusive relationships is the situation's complexity. It's not enough to offer simple instructions like telling the abused person, "You need to get out." It's not that simple. The person has to come into their own consciousness and reach their own awareness.

They may be completely unconscious, thinking, 'Well, they'll stop. If I just change the way I am, they'll stop acting the way they are.'

But no, it has nothing to do with you. Even though they're telling you it has everything to do with you. The whole situation is about what you do and what you don't do.

The thing to keep in mind is not to succumb to isolation. Seeking support from others is essential to gaining clarity and understanding what is truly normal and beneficial.

Disconnecting from others leaves one without the perspective needed to navigate a path to safety and well-being.

It's time to start being un-oblivious.

Unaffected

I have gone through several serious challenges and experiences in my life, and they have affected me in ways that have made me stronger, not weaker.

These trials have strengthened my sense of self, my resolve, and my understanding of my own sense of reality. I no longer rely on other people's sense of reality, and I recognize that there is more than one reality.

In abusive relationships, people may use 'gaslighting' to manipulate your perception and convince you that your reality is wrong, and their reality is right and what you need to believe.

That's exactly what happened to me in my relationship. It's a tactic abusive people use when in a relationship.

Despite my own confusion, I had an inkling that this wasn't how things were supposed to be, and I trusted my instincts.

Some people choose to remain stuck in the difficulties they face, while others decide not to escape, move on, or compartmentalize their feelings.

Alternatively, they may resort to numbing themselves with drugs, alcohol, sex, shopping, video games, pornography, or even immersing themselves in their business or being an activist. On the contrary, they may succeed at work but find the rest of their lives in shambles.

It's important to recognize when something terrible has happened, and it stopped because you took the initiative to change it.

You learn that you have the ability to recognize when things aren't right, and that you have the power to escape and rebuild your life.

Once you understand that you have this ability to go beyond the expectations that people have of you, you can begin to live a life that is truly free from the shackles of abuse.

It happened to me, and although it affected me and challenged me in many ways, it made my life better once I got over it.

It also helps to know that there are people

who are out to do terrible things. You are no longer naive. Living with the belief that everyone has good intentions is not in your best interest, and it is simply not true.

If you go through life like that, you're more likely to become the target of someone who wants to do you harm because you're not paying attention.

I don't live my life as if someone like my ex is going to come back into my life any day. However, I'm aware that people like that exist.

And I'm going to pay more attention to what my little 'danger, danger' alarm system is telling me.

I won't let it restrict and limit my life, but it will keep me alert, aware, and careful. It's not an easy task and requires constant practice to balance.

As long as you're alive, you can keep honing this skill.

Undestroyed

Undeterred, even in the face of life's most

formidable trials, the indestructible will rise from the depths of adversity with unwavering strength and resilience.

On the medical side, I have personally experienced the debilitating effects of the encephalitis I contracted after receiving the MMR vaccine at age six, which resulted in a coma and paralysis.

It took me two years of rehabilitation to regain my ability to walk, talk, and do everything I used to do. But I was not the same. I had muscle and nerve damage on the left side of my body. I also have a learning disability, now referred to as 'neurodivergence.'

Although I hide it well, I have a slight speech impediment due to the difference in my ability to move my mouth in the same way on both sides.

Still, I make my living as a public speaker, and I haven't let that hold me back.

Encephalitis changed my physical body, but it didn't destroy my whole being. As a child, I developed so much tenacity that I didn't let anything hold me back, even in a wheelchair.

And even when I was in leg braces and on crutches, when kids would push me or try to bully me in any way, I wouldn't let it get to me.

Far from destroying me, the encephalitis was probably the reason I'm so tough now.

From what I've heard from family members, I wasn't an assertive kid before the encephalitis. So not only did it not destroy me, but it gave me a whole new chance at a different life, and a good one at that.

Such traumatic or difficult events in our lives give us the opportunity to look deeper within and access the deeper wisdom of what is really happening.

What is the incident?

What kind of person is involved?

What lessons can we learn?

Even if it's painful, there's always an opportunity to learn and connect with a deeper wisdom that will eventually help us move forward in life.

It's not realistic to expect instant introspection. When we are faced with an emergency, such as being held at gunpoint, we must first process the terror. It's not two minutes later that we say, 'What was the deeper wisdom in that?'

There are different levels or cycles of grief when you're coming out of that experience. Immediately, your body is flooded with chemicals, and you have to process it all. Similar scenarios, like car accidents, require a period of processing.

Clinically speaking, you can have acute stress disorder for 30 days. It's not post-traumatic stress if you get over it in 30 days.

Most people get over trauma within 30 days. They call it the adjustment period. Beyond that, if people don't adjust to new circumstances within 30 days and instead bury their heads in the sand, avoiding, then they're not processing, and now they have an adjustment disorder.

So it's critical to find a way to get people to start processing what just happened as soon as possible, within a couple of days.

There are individuals who embody this third option of not being destroyed. They live their lives without seeking attention on social media or constantly tooting their own horns.

They live these principles and hopefully pass them on to those closest to them. However, some may not want to or haven't yet made the commitment to share these ideas more broadly.

———

Personally, I wish more people would embrace the concept of "change your thinking, change your life," attributed to American philosopher Ernest Holmes.

It emphasizes the power of our thoughts and experiences to shape our reactions and responses.

Your thinking shapes your life.

It's about framing your thoughts, how you perceive things, and the words you use to describe your experiences, influencing your reactions and responses. So your mind aligns with these patterns.

For example, if I dwell on disaster, terror, and fear, I'll end up living in that negative state because that's what I'm feeding my mind.

I also have the option of focusing on positivity and believing that everything is good, and I'm safe wherever I go.

Both extremes are unhealthy. A balanced perspective is what you need.

Independence frees us from victimhood.

It gives us the power of choice in the face of life's challenges.

When you're independent, you stop seeing yourself as a victim. Life may continue to throw you difficult curveballs, but you draw strength from your past triumphs.

You know you have choices.

You don't go through life feeling like a victim of your circumstances.

Instead, you go about overcoming obstacles. You know that shitty things are bound to happen from time to time, and you are more confident that you can get through them.

When you're independent, you have what's called an 'internal locus of control,' a clinical term that means your moral compass is within you.

You don't navigate your life by other people's compasses. You have your own compass. That's what independence is.

I grew up with my father telling me these stories over and over again. To be independent is to know yourself. As a Western principle, it means you research, you reflect, you write in your journal, or you ask people for feedback.

In the workplace, they do it with something called 360-degree feedback. Asking the people you report to, report to you and your peers, for feedback. You can take it in, and while you can get valuable insights from it, it is not going to replace your own sense of knowing and your own compass.

However, you also understand that even compasses are fallible. You're not oblivious to the fact that our compasses can sometimes lead us off course.

That doesn't mean you've already failed. Sometimes it's just a redirection. Or you can accept that failure and come to terms with it as a fact of life.

Embracing independence means accepting that life includes both success and failure.

Success is not a constant state, but a fleeting experience.

There is no such thing as attaining nothing but success, just as, from the Buddhist perspective of enlightenment, enlightenment is not a permanent, indefinite state of being.

As the old stories go, you put down the heavy sack, you breathe, and you notice the beautiful horizon.

Then you bend down, you pick up the heavy sack, and you walk on.

That's the visual image of enlightenment.

That's the independence I want. What about you?

NON-THEIST

Most people think of themselves or others as being believers or non-believers, meaning theists or atheists. Others will use words like agnostic, which means 'I'm not sure.'

I like 'non-theist' because a non-theist isn't really taking a position.

It's not saying "I'm uncertain." It's more saying, "It's not the most important thing."

I learned about this concept of non-theism from the Dalai Lama, the Tibetan spiritual leader. When somebody asked him, "What is your religion?" He said it was compassion and that he was a non-theist.

Tibetan Buddhism is a very particular kind of Buddhism that combines the Lama-ism of Tibet with the Buddhism of India.

Buddhism is the middle path between the indulgences of the Brahmin caste in which Siddhartha, The Buddha, was raised, and his experience with the Jains who are ascetic, quite restrictive, in all of their activities.

Buddhism is that middle path between luxurious opulence and asceticism, which can be eating just a grain of rice at a time, wearing the same tunic every day, begging for alms (ex. money, food, or clothing), and sweeping the road in front of you as you walk so that you don't inadvertently kill a living thing: step on a bug.

_____

Whenever I encounter atheists, they have a fervor for their fundamentalist position that equals the most fundamentalist Christians.

I'm not saying this is all atheists, but all the atheists that I have met and known were involved in some sort of organized religion at one point in their life. Then they were disappointed, excommunicated, shunned, or made to feel unwelcome in some way, often because of sexual orientation and/or gender expression issues.

Their response was to reject the whole system outright, not just the person in the congregation who rejected them or the teachings of that one particular minister, or the particular Protestant or Catholic denomination. They reject Christianity outright, this huge system of thought, cultural system, and meaning-making system for large swaths of people around the world, and very much so historically.

And so I think what happens is they get personally hurt. They might feel betrayed by their religion or their religious leaders or God, and their response is to reject it all.

I understand the reaction. But to a certain degree, I think if it persists, it's a bit childish.

It's sort of like when a child says, "I'm never talking to you again," to their parents.

It makes short term sense for people who are struggling to come to terms with it. But if they are a person of faith, and they want to belong to something, and fellowship is really important to them, why are they throwing the baby out with the bath water?

Now they feel ostracized, marginalized, dejected, rejected, and demoralized.

Over the course of time, days, weeks, months, years, and decades, a person realizes there's a lot of life that they've missed out on because they haven't been in fellowship or communion with people.

Being an entirely rational, argumentative style communicator, taking positions from the atheist point of view, has created for them a different sort of isolation and alienation and rejection from their family members, friends, and peer group.

But let's think about the third space here, again. There are a lot of options you can choose, for how you would like to orient your life with regard to religion, spirituality, and fellowship.

If a person is attending a particular denominational church, let's just stick with Protestant, and the message they hear from the pulpit, from the congregation, or from the larger body of the church, doesn't resonate with them, the options are pretty unlimited.

They can do what people have done, which is outright reject Christianity, or they can go and find another Protestant denomination that is similarly oriented towards theirs, and they can try that out and see if its a better fit. Because there are what are referred to as open, welcoming, celebrating, inclusive houses of worship that are part of Protestant denominations.

So if they want to hold on to being a person who is a theist, then they can do it in that way.

They can also abandon Christianity if they'd like, but then they can take up Zoroastrianism. They can take classes on Kabbalah. They can go off to some of the new-age versions of Protestantism, like the Church of Religious Science or Unity. They could go and become a Unitarian Universalist, or a Humanist, or check out all the varieties of Buddhism that exist, and go and learn some mindfulness, and take up meditation practices.

But the anger that sets in at this rejection, at this betrayal, creates an angry response. And

I've got to tell you, I've never met a happy atheist.

Have you? A 'happy-go-lucky', 'you do you, I do me' atheist?

They're often rigid in their thinking about not just religion, but a lot of other things in their life, and they're very argumentative. And I think that happiness is one of the points for being alive, for living.

Am I saying we should all believe in God? Gosh, no. What I'm saying is that you've got to get your happiness somewhere. My atheist friends don't seem all that happy.

We live in a society where people have grown up in homes where there's a lot of instability and uncertainty.

And when there's instability and uncertainty, we question things like, "How do we orient ourselves?", "Where's the compass?", and a lot of people use religion for that compass.

Other people use nature or the natural world

as their compass. And still others use their ethical guiding system as that compass.

But I do believe that there are certain people who for one reason or another are without a compass. They're kind of bouncing around without a sense of self, without being grounded or tethered to people, to a system, to something that keeps them feeling grounded.

If you veer outside the expectation of far-left progressives, or far-right conservatives, you get targeted. And it's the same with religion. If you're part of a very rigid system, like Jehovah's Witnesses, you're not allowed to be curious about your faith.

Certain sects of Islam are the same way. You can't be curious about things. You must adhere to the teachings.

That's not to say that there aren't very liberal and moderate members of those religions. But the more rules there are, the harder it is to be curious and step outside and test those boundaries.

Non-theism isn't completely without rules.

Non-theism just means that there's more flexibility in the rules and that they allow a lot more questioning, curiosity, and hypothesis testing. And open dialogue with other people.

Non-theism can contain rules, but not limits. So in these other systems, they have rules and limits. They have dogma. One of the factors of non-theism is probably that people who are non-theistic, but not atheistic, are people who aren't taking positions on whether theism or atheism is right or wrong or good or bad. It's staying open-minded and curious about that as well.

A dogma imposes limits on what people can do, what people can think, what people can believe. With non-theism, it's about being non-dogmatic, but there are religions or denominations, for example, 'Unitarian Universalist' is a version of a Protestant religion or denomination that does not have a dogma.

The thing about Unitarian Universalism is that everybody in your given church isn't all the same as you. They can be a Humanist, an atheist, nontheist, agnostic, a Buddhist, a Jew, or a Christian. They don't put limits on who may worship. Whereas in Catholicism, you can only take communion if you've been baptized. It's a rigid, fixed limitation. Unitarians don't have things like that.

Non-theism is important for me because I want to be able to live my life being curious, open, and interested in all kinds of different spiritual and religious systems and traditions.

So, for example, I enjoy going to a variety of worship services and meetings for a number of different kinds of religions. I like reading texts written by practitioners of those religions. I like reading the religion's noted books.

When I was in seminary, I took classes on Hinduism, Buddhism, Islam, Christianity, Catholicism, and Judaism. I want to be open to learning all of that, and experiencing it, going to the Hare Krishna temple and hanging out with the Baha'is.

When I think about dumpster divers, they go through and look for the treasures (ex. clothing, furniture, food). They're gleaning.

What I do is a type of gleaning. I'm searching for what Ken Wilbur calls 'perennial wisdom.'

I'm limited, of course, because I've mostly only studied Eastern and Western religions and philosophies. I don't know much about some of the traditions that might be more indigenous to Africa or South America, for example.

When I was younger, my father gave me a book called 'The Four Agreements,' and whether it's fictional or not, I believe that's based on a system espoused by the Toltecs, which were an indigenous group in central Mexico. It's a whole system of thinking.

The Toltec teachings are not something that I would have learned in my Catholic Catechism classes as a child. So it's a matter of opening my mind to different ways of seeing the world, different ways of seeing people, different ways of figuring out how to resolve conflicts, and it makes it possible to learn.

It also creates a sense of humility because if I think I have the right answer for something, it's likely that I'm going to encounter additional answers to the same situation.

And then I have to come to terms with, "Well, does my answer work best for me in my circumstances?"

If your system is working for you, then keep with it.

If your system is not working for you, seek something else.

What I like about being non-theist is that it gives me the opportunity to ask questions and wrestle with the answers, to seek out new and different information from different systems of belief, thought, philosophy, and religion.

Unlimited Options

Limitations are placed on individuals from a young age, based on the family they're raised in and the culture they're living in.

First it goes like this, 'there are certain things you don't do, you don't say'. And then, 'there are certain things that you must do.'

And so there are these limitations, and as we get older, we have the opportunity to step outside of them, and go beyond them.

Not everybody does. Some people like the limitations and stick within them.

Some people grow up in the Amish faith and remain there their entire lives because they like that system, and it works for them. But they give their young people an option at a certain age to go out and live in the world among 'the English' (non-Amish) for a year, and then when they come back, they dedicate their lives to that community. I think that's a wonderful way to consider a commitment to a faith tradition.

As if to say, 'We think we've got something really good here, but we're going to give you an opportunity to check out what else is going on and see what you want to do, and then you can come back if you want.'

I can get behind that way of operating society. Give kids an option to choose their path.

Give them some control.

Meaning-Making

Some people get anxious just going into the supermarket because there are so many different options. For example, I'm struck by all the different kinds of Cheerios available now.

If you're raised in a system, let's say Catholicism, and "this is how you make meaning of life," "this is how you make decisions," "this is who you spend time with," it's your whole life, all in one package.

But, that can be a bit limiting. That's limiting in the places where you can get meaning, and where you can have your own ideas.

Non-theism allows for meaning-making, incorporating ideas and concepts from a wider range of possibilities. Because if one is non-theist, they can incorporate into their meaning-making something that is coming out of the Jain system, and incorporating that in with something that's from the Bhakti part of Hinduism, which is focused on love, or something even from Christianity.

You're not limited to just your prepackaged system. With non-theism, meaning-making is more like going to a buffet than being served off of a menu that only has one option for appetizer, entrée, and dessert.

More entrenched or inflexible systems offer safety and security, that's part of the package. And so, if you're entrenched in that, it's very difficult to move out of it, because it feels unsafe and insecure to do so.

But it's conditional because if you start asking too many questions or making contrary assertions, it can cause you to be exiled, excommunicated, and shunned.

Whereas in non-theism, who's going to do that? Who's going to exile you from non-theism?

You never have to set foot in any place of worship.

You're not an adherent to it, you're not a member signing the document that says, "I believe this and that."

There's no creed. Just meaning-making.

Non-Dogmatic

Non-theism is non-dogmatic because there's no enforced beliefs, no creed, and nothing you have to sign or utter to demonstrate adherence.

There's nothing you have to say, no particular postulation of the body that you need to do, no responsibility to proselytize, and there are no specific rituals that are part of non-theism.

A non-theistic person can celebrate Christmas and go to a Seder. They're free to do whatever they want, as long as they are respectful of other's traditions and can find people that are willing to let them be part of their rituals.

And thankfully, there are lots of different people like that who are welcoming in that way, into their homes or into their places of worship. So it's non-dogmatic in that way.

Also, the ability to gain knowledge, information, and experience from a variety of sources naturally builds a non-dogmatic frame of thinking.

That's not to say that there could be people,

I haven't met them yet, who become pretty dogmatic in their non-theism.

My first curiosity about a person like that would be, 'Are they really an atheist, and they're calling themselves non-theist?'

The second is, 'Is it just a reaction against something?'

Anything is possible, but I think it's less possible for a non-theist to be dogmatic because of how flexible, fluid, dynamic, and somewhat limitless non-theism is.

If you think about it, there are people who might claim to be non-theists, who like to talk about being a Pastafarian and how they worship the big spaghetti monster in the sky. It's totally made up.

Or some people who call themselves Jedis.

Jediism is one of the more popular options outside major religions. It is a very popular choice in the United States, and in England. Many people actually select Jediism, from the Star Wars movies, as their religion in the US 2000 Decennial Census.

So I think there are people who are having fun with it. I'd say those people are probably non-theistic, but I don't know if they espouse non-theism.

Well, 'may the force be with you,' I guess.

Perennial Gleaning

'Perennial Wisdom for the Spiritually Independent' is the title of a book by Richard Rohr I read many years ago. It's this concept that within all the major religious systems in the world, there are commonalities.

Not the history of the religion, not the polity of it, not the creed, but what it is basically, at its heart.

And so in Christianity, it's the golden rule to "treat people as you'd want to be treated."

And the Platonist says, "Treat them how they want to be treated."

Perennial wisdom says that in all major world religions, there's something, some idea or concept that's similar in all of them.

If you're not associated very tightly with another system, you have the freedom to go and read other books, listen to other sermons or messages, attend other services, and meet with other people of faith.

And from that, you can glean ideas, and wisdom, and then you figure out what you're going to take and what are you going to leave.

You have the option to say, "Yeah, that works for me," or "No, that doesn't work for me."

And then maybe a year or two later you pick that one idea, concept, or ritual back up and think, 'It fits with my life now.'

You're not held to one particular set of beliefs your entire life.

––––––––––

The concept of gleaning comes from picking over the fields after they've been harvested.

There's a lot that's left behind, so the poor would go and glean from the fields.

The way the word is now used is not as drastic as that. I think of it more like the dumpster divers or the free-gans these days, the people who are looking for free stuff.

What I'm recommending to you, in a non-theist way, is similar to that because you're picking and choosing what you want to take with you.

You're looking at it, listening to it, and you're considering, 'How does this fit or not fit into my way of living, thinking, and believing? Does it complement it? Does it augment it? Does it replace it?'

It's like constantly being open to sifting, filtering and shuffling things around based on life experiences.

It's similar to conflict management. There are different systems of thought around conflict management, but most people would agree that there are four different ways that people respond to conflict.

They compete, compromise, collaborate, or they completely hide from it.

And so most people have a primary way they deal with conflict when conflict arises in their life. But they also have a secondary, and maybe a tertiary way. We can learn how to reorient ourselves to how to respond to conflict.

Not one way of responding to conflict is bet-

ter than the other. It depends on the circumstances, on the people, and on the outcome
that is sought.

In some cases, you want to be very competi-
tive in what you're going after and in others,
you want to collaborate.

Sometimes, compromise is going to get you
where you need to go, maybe just in the short
term, but it gets you past any barriers, and it
keeps relationships more intact.

Curiosity, openness, and flexibility, those are
good prerequisites.

People who aren't curious, aren't open, and
aren't flexible are less likely to find themselves in this realm because it's too far outside that mindset.

Am I the Jesus of non-theism? No. But, from
a different tradition, if you think of Jesus as a
teacher, then okay. But I'm not a prophet.

I'd say that the Dalai Lama is a prophet of
non-theism. He's the head of the Tibetan

Buddhist Church and has lived in exile for most of his life.

He says that his religion is compassion. If your religion is compassion, that's not theistic because it has nothing to do with the supernatural or a deity.

I like that. That's another thing, people can orient themselves towards their religion as compassion, forgiveness, or equanimity (psychological stability).

You can make the highest value in your life be something like a quality, a characteristic that spans beyond just you, the person.

What is the pearl to be found within non-theism? There's a phrase that comes to mind from Christian scripture (John 14:15-21), and sung by Marvin Gaye, "Let your conscience be your guide."

When you're a theist, your guide is not your conscience, it's the religion. It's whatever that has come down through tradition, it's the scripture.

On the other hand, atheism is the rejection of religion. It's the internal locus of control, having your own moral compass where you orient yourself based on your own thoughts and beliefs on things as long as they're not harmful to you or other people.

I trust my own sense of self, my capacity to take in lots of different kinds of information and process it, accept what I want to accept and reject what I want to reject and be open to the possibility that down the line I might slough off some of the things that I've taken on and pick up some new things.

My way of thinking and believing, my values, ethics, and morals may appear inconsistent over the arc of my life, but that's only because new information has come in. It was Ralph Waldo Emerson, who was very critical of this application of consistency.

If from the time we're young until the time we die, we remain very consistent, there's something about being an independent individual that's lacking in that.

Emerson was a Unitarian Universalist Minister, and while reciting a sermon that he had written many years before, out loud to a graduating class at Harvard Divinity School back in the 1800s he got to a place where he stopped, took a pencil, and he scratched out a passage saying, "Oh, I don't believe that anymore."

Later, he wrote , "A foolish consistency is the hobgoblin of little minds."

So this idea is that I'm not beholden even to my own ethics, morals, and values if they fail to serve me, to bring happiness and joy to my life, to help me make meaning of things, to stay open versus being forced or limited in what I can value, what I can believe, and what I can think.

Screw the hobgoblins.

DIPLOMATIC

For me, being diplomatic is about finding ways to build bridges between people, individuals, or groups of people. Not in an individual sense, but in the larger context between organizations.

A diplomat is a person who's going and doing diplomacy, and diplomatic work, as a career. That is a way of describing diplomacy and being diplomatic.

When I think about it in the interpersonal realm, I think of being a diplomat or diplomacy as cultural humility, in the sense that one can probably never gain full competency in ideas, cultures, and experiences that are outside their own, but we can gain a sense of humility about other people's cultures and their experiences.

And when we do that, we can develop a vocabulary that gives us the opportunity to speak to people using words that they recognize, and that resonate with them.

So for example, if I was going to have a conversation with somebody from a different country than mine, I'm going to be very careful not to use American slang terms when I talk to them. I'm going to make sure that I am explaining the words that I use in a way that isn't dumbing it down or making it seem as if the person is a child and can't comprehend.

I'm just going to take into consideration that there are differences in expressions between languages and between cultures. So that's one way.

I take to heart this concept of 'agree to disagree,' but I go a little bit further than that. It's not my goal to change another person's mind about something that they hold very dear to them, for whatever reason.

Now it's true that they or I or others may

come to a change of mind, but it's not going to come through force. The only way one changes their mind about something through force is if they're being coerced into it. (Stockholm syndrome is a version of that.)

In social work, we call it meeting people where they are.

Who are they? Where have they come from? What have they been through?

Then it's about eliciting important information, rather than launching into my proscriptive or prescriptive ideas about how they can improve their life, or they can make things better.

I might have an idea that if you get some great nights of sleep several days in a row, your life is probably going to work out a little better for you in the short term and maybe long term, but I'm not going to just tell them that directly. Unless I am teaching a sleep well-being course, which I regularly do.

You have to find a way to ease into things, to talk about things in a way that gets the information past the barriers that we all have in our mind, that stops information that we don't want coming in.

My general understanding of diplomacy is that there is an intention. I could be wrong, but I believe there is an intention on behalf of the nation-state, the government, or whoever is engaging in diplomacy, to come to an agreement with the other party or parties for some sort of change to take place.

You're coming to the table, you're going through a negotiation process. There's a lot of back and forth, you're striving for a resolution to whatever the conflict is. I think that can be optimum in a lot of cases, but not always.

Let me give you an example. When you're a therapist working with somebody who is in a violent relationship, or they have a violent marriage, it doesn't work to say to the person, "You need to leave," or ask them, "Why haven't you left?"

That is too abrupt. It's too startling. They are dealing with guilt, shame and confusion. They may feel paralyzed emotionally, physically, and financially.

If we want to really meet people where they are, we have to find where they're at, mentally and emotionally, and the only way to do that is to elicit information, ask questions.

So I think, generally speaking, traditional diplomacy is going in with a set idea, or a set of ideas, that we think will fix the problem, solve the issue, settle the case, or get people to come to agreement on something.

I take the position of, "I don't know." I have uncertainty about what's really going on and what might be the good solution or good agreement or good prospect for that other individual if we're talking interpersonally or those individuals.

So I'm going to elicit information from those individuals before jumping into, if ever, a prescriptive form of telling people what they need to do.

If we're talking about the third space, the prescriptive is on one side, and the elective is in the middle.

What's on one side would be taking the stance, 'I'm not going to get involved. That's their own personal business. It's not worth the risk. I wouldn't know what to say.' So it's avoidance. It's avoidance of having a deep or meaningful, useful, helpful kind of conversation with the person. That's not good either.

———

One tool to be diplomatic, in a good way, is stripping down any words from my language that could be misconstrued. So not using words that one might see on a regular basis on their social media platforms, or words that people might encounter when they're going through diversity training programs, or words that they might encounter in their religious home, or in their places of worship.

I try to find a way to speak as plainly as possible, but not to a child's level of discourse, either. Just speaking as plainly as possible in adult language about what I'm having a conversation with somebody about.

Also, I tend to take the reference point of, 'I lack information'. Because I might have information on a particular topic that I'm having a discussion with somebody about, but not enough.

How could I ever have enough? I think it's my sense of lack of certainty that helps with diplomacy. Because if I feel like I'm certain about something, then I'm going to be more strident in the way I speak with people, I'm going to be more insistent, I'm going to be impatient, and I'm going to be argumentative.

I want to be none of those things when I want to have an actual full, deep, meaningful, impactful kind of dialogue with somebody.

I want to be able to pay attention to the words that I use, because what ends up happening is, if I'm having a conversation with somebody, and I say, DEI, diversity, equity, inclusion, there are certain people who are going to hear that phrasing and immediately put up the red light to me in their mind. They're going to resist whatever comes next because they think I'm a culprit of some ideology.

On the other side, people are going to hear that, and they're going to make up their minds about me in a different direction. When all I'm doing is just using shorthand for common concepts or words.

So I have to find a way to talk about issues that people are less familiar with hearing. Or terms they're less familiar with hearing associated with the topic that we're discussing.

So, as I've mentioned before in the book, I like to 'play dumb'. What that means is I ask a lot of questions. And what I'm trying to do is elicit from them by asking questions rather than making statements, because it gets around people's cognitive filters.

If we ask a question, especially in a way that's not riddled with these filtered-out terms that people might hear, it's going to elicit from somebody a more genuine, perhaps a more heartfelt, unscripted, and unrehearsed response.

Being diplomatic also entails putting aside grievances and desired outcomes and coming to the table, so to speak, with a variety of different people to find either common ground or core values.

If you are having a negative response to the polarization that you see in your government, locally and nationally, coming together with other people and finding out what values we share, and what things we have in common gets us past polarization.

That doesn't mean we have to agree with each other. It just means that we can understand each other better so that when we get together with family or when we're with a group of friends that we've known for years, all of a sudden, all the rifts that have been happening over the last few years between those groups of people, we can find a way back to whatever connections we had with them.

Freedom from Aggravation

Within the last year, I was contacted by a person that I've known since I was 14 years old. And they wrote to tell me how disappointed they were in me.

I haven't heard from them in a couple of years, but they thought they'd reach out to me and tell me how disappointed they were in me because I was taking such a middle of the road tactic and talking about things that have to do with transgender people and identity and politics.

I took the time to read their message multiple times, and then I also took the time to respond in a way where I didn't come off as defensive, I didn't come off as making excuses, I didn't come off as flippant, and I didn't come off as irritated.

I ran it past my wife, who's probably the most diplomatic person I know, and she gave me the thumbs up and said, "I don't see how anybody could find fault with that."

But this person found fault with it because they said it sounded like "a form letter that I would just copy and paste and send to anybody who criticizes me," because it was so well crafted.

They said, "I had some other people look at it, and they said, it just sounds like a form letter. It's not genuine."

And I wrote back, and I said, "Well, you are correct. I did take time to lay out my thoughts," because I hadn't really thought about her perspective much previously.

So, eventually I just had to let this person

go. This is a person who had been in and out of my life since I was 14. And, to be honest, sometimes our connection had been good and sometimes it had been bad.

So I thought about it, and then decided to sever the relationship.

Being diplomatic isn't something that's going to work 100% of the time, but I'd say it's worth trying 100% of the time.

So when it doesn't work, we have to make a decision to either physically or metaphorically push back from the table and walk away.

And we have to decide, are we making a commitment to come back to the table, come back to the person, come back to the discussion, or are we making the decision that there have been so many attempts to work it out that sometimes we just need to go in a different direction?

What would be the point of retaining that connection with that person at that point? What would we talk about?

If they were the kind of person that could put that one issue aside, but all the other connections that we have over the course of our lifetime could still just kind of go forward, talking about our family, talking about work. But no, that wasn't possible for them.

What I got from severing that relationship was freedom from the ongoing work of maintaining a tenuous connection.

Freedom from the aggravation.

Gender Neutral?

Recently I was invited to moderate a discussion between two groups of people who seemingly hold very different views on a topic.

I'd say one set of these people were what you would call 'gender critical'. People who are gender critical believe that there's something called 'gender ideology'.

Gender ideology, they say, shows up in our society, here in the States, but probably globally, in the lessons that are being taught to children about same-sex relationships, the social constructivist notion of biological sex, and gender identity being a spectrum.

And then on the other side, you'd have what would be called 'gender-affirming' individuals. And there's a spectrum of gender-critical views and there's a spectrum of gender-affirming views.

Gender-affirming people tend to subscribe to, believe in, and advocate for people of all ages, minors, children, adolescents, and adults, to gain access to what they would call medically-necessary life-saving medical care to treat gender dysphoria.

Whereas, gender-critical people are going to mostly be against that for children and adolescents. They advocate to wait until you're 18 or 25. And the more extreme gender critics don't want anybody to ever get access to gender-related medical care. Or they might not even believe there's such a thing as being transgender or transsexual.

So I was invited to be the moderator for a group who hold these two viewpoints. I would periodically bring all of them together, pose a question to the group, and have them answer from their perspective. Then we would have a dialogue and see if there was any common ground, any core values, or both.

It's actually been very successful. And the groups of people are not just random people. On both sides of this issue, these would be considered leaders within that community, so to speak.

It was an honor and a privilege to be asked to moderate these dialogues.

I know people from both sides of the issue. I've mostly spent my time on the gender-affirming side, but I know a lot of people on the gender-critical side. I land more in the middle between the extremes of each viewpoint.

I get a sense of accomplishment from moderating these panels, but also a level of satisfaction that my life experiences, my academic studies, my work experience, and my philosophy of life, so to speak, have brought me to this place.

There's so much conflict going on around the Western world, at least, on this very topic right now with transgender stuff.

People are taking very entrenched positions, and they're getting into bitter fights online about this. People are losing sleep and jobs.

I wish these individuals, who are considered leaders in these two communities, would be willing to craft a joint statement that would go out to the world to try and tone down this polarization, this infighting that's been happening.

But many on both sides say that, even sitting down and having a discussion with somebody from the 'gender critical camp' or 'gender-affirming camp' is tantamount to acceptance of their views as legitimate.

It's tantamount to betrayal, to heresy. Because it's enforced like religious dogma.

So let's change that, and have a conversation.

Conversation

One of the ways I am diplomatic in my marriage is I don't have an expectation that my wife is going to suddenly become a totally different person, or that all of a sudden she's going to behave in a way that accords with my specific desires and wishes.

I met her as she is, and we decided to marry as two individuals, and we remain those individuals.

We do things very differently. We have different ideas about things. We take different positions on issues.

But we have spent the last 21 years together, with these differences being obvious from the very beginning, and never once have our differences risen to the level of a heated argument that led to shouting or name-calling or total despair over the marriage, or contemplation of divorce. Never.

Because one of the things we did early on is we attended couples workshops where we learned how to communicate with each other.

Recently, we were having a discussion about how in Florida, our medical board and our osteopathic board created new informed consent forms for people who were going through medical gender transition.

There are forms for adults, forms for minors, forms for masculinizing hormones, feminizing hormones, and puberty-blocking hormones. They're 10 to 13 pages long, they're very long informed consent forms.

And we were having a discussion about it, I said, "Oh, I think that this is going to make people stop and think about the outcomes of their treatment, both what they like and don't like, what they want and don't want."

I was saying, "What are the medical contra-indications of taking certain medications? Because you have to initial everything at the end of each page, it's quite spelled out. And there's a lot of talk in there about mental health services."

My wife was of the mind that people wouldn't read the forms thoroughly. That they'd just initial them and move on. So it won't actually do what they want, which is to inform patients.

And I said, "Well, but the doctors who are prescribing the medication are supposed to go over the form with the patient."

Now, neither one of us is certain that doctors will actually do that. We're of two minds as to the efficacy of an informed consent document that is so robust.

As we were trailing off from the conversation, I said, "Well, time will tell."

Time will tell because this is brand new. If anybody has even started this process yet, they're ahead of the game. The forms just came out. So, time will tell because right now we're in what's called a temporary or emergency ruling. So, it's going to be about six months before it all sort of plays out, and it'll be interesting to see.

We'll see what happens in six months. My wife is a marriage and family therapist, she works with teenagers as young as 13. Some of them do have gender dysphoria, or they describe themselves as having gender distress or identifying as some kind of trans person, whereas I have never worked with kids or teens as a psychotherapist.

She has a different outlook. I value her perspective because she actually works with that population.

I didn't just make bold statements like, "This is what's going to happen," or, "You're wrong." Either did she.

We don't talk to each other that way. But I also did what I would call 'kick the can down the road.' Time will tell. We'll see in time.

And that just sort of gives the indicator at that point, like, "We can move on in our conversation now. We don't have to keep talking about this."

What I got was an opportunity to have a really wonderful conversation with my wife about an important topic that impacts us both in our different lines of work and personal lives.

We're both of the same mind that informed consent is important, it is being under done, and we need to make sure that it's being done right. But I'm a bit more sure that the new Florida informed consent forms will do that, and she's less certain that they will.

So neither one of us is fully certain.

It might sound hokey, but what I got was just another opportunity to strengthen our relationship.

Hope

Recently, I read an article on Substack that was written for a group of people who have children who are disclosing to their parents, "I'm trans," or, "I'm not your daughter, I'm your son," or, "I have a gender dysphoria, call me this pronoun now."

These parents don't like it. They're very upset about it. They have this platform and they write articles. I subscribe to it because I want to read what parents are concerned about.

Somebody I know wrote an article, and they were explaining a topic, and they were using words that may have been appropriate for the particular person that they were speaking about, but they weren't especially helpful when speaking in general about the population of trans adults.

So I commented on there by introducing myself and saying that like the person they were speaking about, I'm about the same age, had my transition about the same time, had the same surgeon, went through the same surgery, had similar complications, but it has impacted me very differently, and that it's helpful to know that people have different responses to the adversities in their life. Some people grow stronger from them, and some people are pulled under by them.

So I said, "I want parents to know that if their children do grow up to be adults who are still trans, that there's a bunch of us out here that are living very fulfilling and happy and love-filled lives. We're financially successful."

And this one parent, a mother, wrote back and said, "Your positive stories are not welcome here."

I wrote back, and I said, "Well, as a subscriber to the channel with access to comment, I would hope that I could put my comments in."

And she came back with, "We don't want you here, you're not welcome here."

Nobody else said anything, only she did. And I said something along the lines of, "I understand that for some parents in this group, the circumstances that they/you are living through are very upsetting. It's possible that there are parents in this group that are not as upset or will find themselves being less and less upset as time goes on, and their child doesn't desist but is persistent to an adult transgender identity."

I would hope that just knowing that people like me exist can provide them a sense of relaxation mentally, of hope for their child. That it's not as dire as the original article makes it out to be.

I was asserting myself that a place like Substack is an open forum and that if they don't want somebody like me in there, they should have never accepted my subscription.

It's a public forum, and nobody has kicked me off, nobody has asked me to leave. She told me I was unwelcome, but she's not one of the owners, so to speak, of that Substack channel.

My attempt was to provide the readers of the comment section, after they read that story, a sense of hope for parents, just in case.

Because what they're sharing in that Substack is like horror story after sob story after negative outcome after families breaking up and children cutting off contact with them and losing friends and family because of the position (non-affirming) they're taking with their child.

And my hope is that there's going to be a parent, at least one, hopefully, more than one, who read that comment and will just file it in the back of their mind, and one day in the future, they'll be able to remember and go, "Hey, there was this trans man and he said this thing. I'm going to look him up, or I'm going to go find some other resources."

I was planting a seed of hopefulness for these parents.

My goal was to interrupt, so to speak, that being trans is only a negative thing. It is a diagnostic condition, that's gender dysphoria (DSM V) or transsexualism (ICD 10), but it's more than just that.

My goal for them was the feeling of hopefulness. If that parent remembers my comment and their child does persist into adulthood with a trans identity, they can bring that hopefulness and then come into their relationship with their child and therefore pass it onto their child who's trans, so that they can be more hopeful, so that we have more hopefulness within our community.

We need hopefulness in our community, so it gives me a sense of hopefulness to pass on future hope, even in a place like Substack.

Peace

I'm a registered Independent voter because I don't wholly subscribe to, not the platforms of the Democratic or Republican parties, but more the ethos, the philosophy, or the activism or advocacy that's coming out of people who identify from within those two political parties.

In the past, I was just registered as one or the other because that's the only way I could vote in primaries, because I've lived in States where you have to be a registered Democrat or Republican to vote in the primary. That's the way it is here also in Florida. So you can't be an independent and get to vote in the primaries.

There's not going to be an independent president in my lifetime, probably, so if I want to cast my ballot for one of the candidates in either of those parties to move forward as the presidential candidate for that party, I have to be able to vote in the primary.

Being registered as independent has given me the opportunity to engage in conversation with people who come from those two parties, who were lifelong members of those parties.

I have family members and friends who have been voting straight-ticket Democrat since they were 18 and straight-ticket Republican since they were 18, and I don't value or favor one worldview over the other.

I find things that I appreciate about all those different people. I also have a lot of friends who are Libertarians, which is sort of a type of Independent, but it is its own political party here in the United States. I have had friends who are members of the Green Party and Peace and Freedom Party. I registered with the Green Party at age 18 in California and remained a Green Party supporter for many years.

I don't tend to take sides, and when you don't take sides, some people are going to find you unreliable or unstable or a person they can't trust, untrustworthy.

We're not that divided or polarized, it's just how it looks on social media. But that's part of it. That's part of the issue. A person who takes a really hard stance on being a 'liberal' or more of a 'progressive', even further left than a liberal, only sees bad from the 'conservatives'.

It's only the far-left and far-right that would

have a problem with somebody like me, because I'm not a true believer in their cause.

So I find favor with people that are 'center', 'center-left,' 'center-right', 'classical liberals', and 'moderates'. I think research has shown that that is the majority of people. So I'm not alone.

There's a sense of confidence that I'm not missing the mark somewhere. The way that I'm viewing things isn't egregious.

My views may be considered controversial by people who aren't center, center-left, center-right, or moderate, but I know that there's this whole broad spectrum of people that are somewhere in the vicinity of me politically and that's a lot of people.

I get peace of mind because if I was camped out in the far-right, or the far-left, I would probably be agitated, or angry often.

I would probably not be getting good sleep. I'd probably be a terrible person to be around.

I'd alienate people from my life unless they subscribed exactly to my viewpoints.

So I get peace of mind. I get a good night's sleep.

I'm surrounded by people who appreciate me

and love me and value me. I'm not contributing to any destruction of property or livelihoods.

I'm not calling for anybody to lose their job or be deplatformed, things that have happened to me. I'm not calling for that for anybody, even the people who have extremist views.

I'm not calling for them to be canceled either, or deplatformed or their livelihood to be impacted.

Being diplomatic is not about compromising values. It's not about acquiescing to other people's demands. It's really about holding your own ground, knowing what you value, knowing what your experience has provided for you in your life, and coming to the table, so to speak, with individuals who have very different opinions and different ideas and different experiences and looking for core values or common ground.

We don't need to necessarily compromise. This is more about learning how to collaborate with others.

There are people who would like to be isolationist.

There are people who are going to go live on land that is just theirs. Their family, their cult, their group.

This exists on the left and the right. There are communes that are women-only. They don't want any men on the land. So there are people who are going to do that. They're going to be isolationist, they're going to withdraw from society.

These are very small groups of people. The majority of us have an investment in being part of communities, our neighborhoods, our cities, our states, our nations, our families, and our workplaces.

We want to be in relationship with people, and the only way to be in a good relationship with other people is to work together.

Let's come together from the heart, not the ego.

CHILDLIKE

Being childlike is not being childish. And I think people do conflate those two. To be childish is like throwing temper tantrums. And that's not what I mean by childlike.

What I mean by childlike is the ability to retain, past childhood, a sense of awe and wonder at the mysteries of the universe and the gloriousness of the natural world, and to remain curious about how things work and why things are the way they are.

When you think about a two-year-old who's like, "Why? Why? Why," I'm not like that. I'm not so much of a pest.

But I'm very curious. I asked my wife just yesterday two or three questions about how something worked and why, because she has more of a scientific mind.

Sure, I could go look it up in an encyclopedia or the dictionary, but I enjoy learning from other people, especially people like my father who I used to be able to go to with certain questions.

And my wife and I used to go to her father with questions like this because she'd say, "Oh, I don't know. Let's call my dad."

But we don't have that access to him anymore since he passed away. And my dad has dementia, so he's unable to answer complex questions.

It's just a matter of that awe, wonderment, curiosity, and not being so inflexible or rigid, thinking that you have the answers for everything.

It's about being open to uncertainty, which as a psychotherapist, I can tell you, uncertainty is what drives a lot of people to counseling because it can be anxiety-producing.

I have the ability to deal with a lot of uncertainty without anxiety, at least not crippling anxiety. I might feel that little butterfly feeling in my stomach, which is just adrenaline releasing into my body, giving me extra energy to do whatever it is I need to.

I've talked about this before. When I was 14 years old, I was in an all girls group home in Ramona, California, which is in a rural area of San Diego County. There were between 40 and 50 adolescent girls that were part of this school.

We lived in separate homes, so it was called a group home system, but we were all picked up every morning by a school bus that brought us to a school on what used to be a campground in the mountains. It was very beautiful.

There were a few girls who were given authorization to go to the public high school, but most of us were going to school on the campgrounds.

And so in the home setting, as I mentioned before, we had what were called 'houseparents' And so there were two kinds of houses. There were the regular houses and the ICU or intensive care unit houses.

The intensive care unit houses had two staff members and one stayed awake all night long, whereas, in the regular houses, the houseparent went to sleep at night because they felt like we were less likely to engage in some sort of activity that they needed to be alerted to.

And I spent time in both types of houses, the regular, and the ICU. And one of the houses that I was in, which was one of the regular houses, there was a houseparent, and I'm not exactly sure what her credentials were, it's possible the houseparents were counselors.

One of these houseparents gave me the lyrics on a piece of paper to the song 'Wild World.' by Cat Stevens.

And for anybody who doesn't know that song, the chorus is,

"Oh, baby, baby, it's a wild world

It's hard to get by just upon a smile

Oh, baby, baby, it's a wild world

I'll always remember you like a child, girl"

There's a character in this song that is playful, and is childlike. But there is also a sense of naïveté. Children are less familiar with the world and the goings-on of things, and so they are more naïve.

At that time, I was certainly both childlike and childish. And the differentiation I would make is that my childlike qualities were the fact that I was fascinated by things all the time.

And I was very curious about wanting to learn about different religions and different philosophies, even at that age. I had spent my childhood being introduced, by my parents, to all kinds of religious and philosophical systems. So I was very curious about that.

But I also did things that she thought were really concerning for a 14-year-old. Childish things.

For example, for my birthday that year, I was given a bag of presents from the other girls in the home. They had gone to the grocery store and bought some toys and other items.

There was no Amazon back then, and they weren't going to get permission to go to the mall. So people bought me things like silly putty and a slinky.

This was in the late 70s, early 80s. And one of the girls bought me a baby bottle. I was putting fruit juices and sodas or water into the baby bottle. And I would drink from it. I thought it was just a gag. Like, I just thought it was funny.

But to her, it was signaling that I was underdeveloped, that I was going to have a really difficult time in life because people were going to be able to manipulate me, and take advantage of me.

Adults can easily manipulate and take advantage of children. And she was really worried, because it's a wild world out there, and I was going to be very vulnerable to that because I was naïve in a sense. And to a certain degree, I still am.

I fully embrace the idea that the older we get, the less we know.

The concept of unknowing is more Eastern than Western, as a philosophical underpinning. Generally, people in the West like to be very certain about things.

I'm okay with being uncertain and unknowing, not knowing things. But I think she was worried because she thought that I wouldn't mature, that I would be frozen in this place of childishness because of how childlike I was.

It's a wild world, after all.

An adult version of being childish of throwing a tantrum, would be like being inflexible in thinking when somebody disagrees with you, or if somebody raises a point that you have disagreement with, the reaction is exaggerated.

You resort to screaming and yelling, or the opposite where you go into silent treatment mode, like how a little child would when they refuse to talk to their parents or their teachers or best friend.

So what's happening is your emotional state is dysregulated, and you're overwhelmed with emotion. So you respond to it by either just letting it go, letting those emotions lead you, or you go the opposite direction, which is trying to compress, stifle, or depress, which is where depression comes from. By pressing down on your emotions to not feel them.

The downside is that people who are adults, who are behaving childishly, will alienate other adults who are emotionally mature.

Because emotionally mature adults don't want to spend time with somebody who is behaving like a child, who is refusing to listen to other views on things, who is name-calling, or who is cutting people out of their life.

It's like the little playground squabble between children where one says to the other, "You're not my best friend anymore," and walks away.

As an adult, we have a lot more leniency towards these things with each other, to varying degrees.

I have a pretty broad leniency for 'transgressions' within my friend and family circle.

I have to be betrayed or insulted in an egregious way to completely cut people out of my life. But it has almost never happened. I almost always circle back around to reconnect with people years later. I don't hold grudges. But, people who are childish hold grudges, and they become like playground bullies.

They try to either physically or mentally or emotionally take you out or down, to try to get you ostracized.

———————

I think being childlike is having a sense of awe, being amazed by finding the natural world and technological advancements to be fantastical.

A sense of uncertainty about the supernatural, like a deity, but also like in non-theist, it's not a denial of the existence. That's one form of looking at nature as a demonstration of the awesomeness of something supernatural.

Remaining curious, being able to ask questions about how that works, and why we might need it.

I think it's really important to be curious about things. If we stopped being curious, then I don't know what that means for us as people.

If I was no longer curious, what I would be saying to myself is that I have all the information I need, I'm settled, and there's nothing anybody can say to me that will have any impact on what I think or feel or believe. That I already know all that I need to know.

People today call that narcissistic. It's arrogant to dismiss that there is the possibility of something out there that we don't know yet.

When we're children, we know a lot because we are exposed to very little, but the older we get we're exposed to more and more ideas, people, and concepts. So our lack of knowing only increases with age. It doesn't decrease. People think it's the other way around, but I don't. The concept of unknowing is very Eastern. I'm not sure if it originated with the Taoists or Buddhists or some other philosophical system, but it's definitely a very Eastern concept.

Children will walk up to a total stranger who is overweight and say, "You're fat."

That's not very kind, but at the same time, it's true.

We have to be able to say what's true, but there's a kinder way to say true things. That's part of diplomacy, which is the ability to say true things in a way that isn't meant to hurt people.

I don't want to be seen as a person who is chastising or stigmatizing. There are certain topics that I'm not going to talk about.

There might be things that I say in the privacy of my home that I wouldn't say out in public. There might be activities that I'm part of, but I'm unnamed in those activities because I want to retain a sense of privacy, but also wanting to control how what I do in say in the world, impacts my wife, for instance.

At this age, it's not going to impact my father, or my mother who is deceased, my cousins are grown and can do whatever they want, I'm not really in contact with my siblings for the most part.

At this point, it's my wife that I feel protective of. I don't want whatever I do and say out in the world, to impact her and the work that she does. So I'm careful, but I'm truthful.

That's the difference, somebody who is childish will 'speak their truth', as a form of radical honesty or just being frank, and they'll say something that's very cruel. That's being immature.

I had a girlfriend years and years ago, over 30 years now, who was really annoyed by my childlike behavior. She did not like it at all.

She was much younger than I was, which I didn't know at the time. It's not like I carded people while I was going on dates with them.

We met in college. So I figured we were about the same age, but I should have thought more clearly about it, because I was a non-traditional student (30), and she was a traditional student (18 or 19). But I wasn't thinking about an age difference at the time.

For her, she was young enough that my child likeness was seen as childish. So not everybody is going to find being childlike endearing. And I have faced that, but it hasn't really impacted me much. My wife doesn't mind. Thankfully.

It's like my bounciness, if you recall the Winnie the Pooh characters, the Tigger character was bouncing all the time because he has so much energy, he's happy-go-lucky, and experiencing the world in that way. I resonate with that.

If you haven't read 'The Tao of Pooh', I highly recommend reading it, because it illustrates these different Taoist principles that are in each of the characters. The Pooh is the ultimate Tao, the Tigger character represents the qi, the energy, the life force. And so it's not a negative thing.

But if you read the book, 'Winnie-the-Pooh,' there are certain characters that are annoyed by Tigger. And who's annoyed by Tigger? The rabbit. Who does the rabbit character represent? A more cynical and rigid person.

People who are cynical, a bit more nihilistic, or heavily critical of things are probably not going to like the childlikeness in me because it's so opposite of them. They can't see the good in life and in the world, so how can they be so joyful when all they see is destruction, death, and demise?

In my experience in particular, the upside of

being childlike is that I've never had to deal with debilitating anxiety or depression.

And clearly, that's not because I haven't experienced 'trauma' in my life. I've dealt with a lot of trauma. The first 20 years of my life were basically nonstop trauma of all kinds; medical, physical, sexual, emotional, and financial.

I think it has a lot to do with being introduced to Eastern philosophies in my young life by my father, who gave me the book 'Zen and the Art of Motorcycle Maintenance' when I was 13.

I was taken to get my transcendental meditation mantra for my 12th birthday. I think that that helped plant the seeds.

But we all have a certain temperament. We have a default setting that is very visible to our parents, especially our mothers when we're infants.

They can tell the difference between their kids, right out of the gate, right after you're born, practically.

We have a certain temperament that's default, that's set from birth. For me, with the encephalitis, my temperament was reset.

That's an interesting thing about me. I had a significant personality shift that was noticeable to everyone except me, of course, because I was too little, at six years old, to notice or remember.

I continued with my childlikeness past childhood, but I cast off the childishness at a certain point in my life, probably a little too late. It's possible that into my 20s, I was still behaving in a childish manner because of the brain damage I suffered. So I was a little bit slower to develop my prefrontal cortex, which is what helps us not behave in a childish manner past childhood.

People have asked me over the years, "How can you be so joyous? How can you be so optimistic?"

Well, that's how. Exposure to meditation and retaining my childlike qualities.

———

Another way of describing childlikeness is about being optimistic.

People ask, "How can you have such a sense of awe and wonder when you've not only experienced really terrible things, but you're part of the LGBT community that as a whole community has experienced discrimination and prejudice and all kinds of issues, not just in the United States, but historically outside the States as well and continues to be within and outside the United States?"

How can I do that? Because I'm a whole person.

My sexual orientation, my gender identity, so to speak, and how I present to the world are just facets of me.

I have all these other facets of me. And a large facet of me is this childlikeness that I've never outgrown.

To speak clinically, it's a protective factor, it is a Teflon that protects me from the injustices, and the cruelties.

It's not that I'm not struck deeply by something like the exploitation and sex trafficking of children. That cuts me to my core, but it doesn't sway me off of also having a sense of awe and wonder.

I can contain, I can hold both of these things

simultaneously so that I don't drift too far up into the clouds away from reality, but I also don't succumb and get pulled down by the weight of that reality.

The opposite of childlikeness isn't maturity, I think being childlike is maturity; it's a well-rounded or holistic maturity.

To completely deny, suppress, stigmatize, or chastise the childlikeness of us, as human beings, the playfulness, in a non-religious way, would be a denial of the spirit of the person.

I know that some people feel like so much harm has come to them, and that they cannot find it within themselves to be playful, but they can. They can find their way. But others might have had a childhood with no play, so it's not a way back for them, it's something completely different. It's having to tap into something very, very deep within the self. But that can be difficult and painful.

It would be easy to be childish; being without any filters and having no sense of empathy, no qualms with how other people are feeling about how you're behaving.

It's easy to fake maturity. For example, I was reading a review of a book the other day talking about how there's an emphasis in a lot of societies on manners and etiquette and how you ought to do things, in those places that enforce etiquette and manners.

But those raised in a system where manners and etiquette were the most important thing were lacking civility.

So a person can consider themselves to be mature, but what they really might be saying is "I'm above you," which is arrogance, not maturity.

Individuals from those societies can't differentiate between childlike and childish behaviors, because they were childlike when they were a child, and they think "Why would an adult want to be childlike?"

They dismiss it all as being childish. "You shouldn't have a sense of awe and wonder because we're destroying the planet. The ozone layer is fading away and the planet's heating up, and we're killing a lot of animals to eat them."

They're constantly consumed with all of this negativity. So to them, awe and wonder seem childish and foolhardy.

I think people become quite snide and contemptuous when they make comments like, "I'm an adult," "I'm mature," or "If you're mature, then you don't behave in a childish manner" in response to encountering a childlike adult.

What else do I mean by childish? It's being silly, but not in a stand-up comedy routine kind of silly. Children get really silly and become nonsensical because they can't make sense of a lot of things.

But I'm an adult, I can make sense of things. So I can be playful, but I'm not silly, which the American Heritage Dictionary defines as "exhibiting a lack of good judgment or common sense; foolish. And, lacking seriousness or responsibleness; frivolous."

I can recognize that there's much that I don't know, versus when we're children oftentimes, we think that we know everything because our universe is small. And we say that we know a lot, and parents are just getting in our way, especially in adolescence.

There's a middle place between being a mature curmudgeonly adult, versus a silly child.

It's about being in that between space. The third space.

If an adult was sucking their thumb or throwing a temper tantrum, that's not childlike, that's childish.

That's clearly very different from somebody who enjoys going to playgrounds and swinging on the swings, I enjoy that. It's enjoying and remembering that freedom of flying. A lot of adults don't take the time or don't feel like it'd be appropriate to take the time to play.

Why not? Play, have fun.

Having fun is hard for people when they're focused on either their own misery, or they're focused externally on all the miseries in the world.

So somewhere in between being focused on the misery of the self, and misery in the world, is a place of saying, "Yeah, there are a lot of really unfortunate things going on in the world globally, nationally, regionally, locally. But there's still an opportunity to find a time to play."

Just like a kid will hide under the covers when they're overwhelmed, adults might compartmentalize to depress their innate feelings of frustration or anxiety.

So it's in that middle place where we can recognize, 'This is unfortunate. I wish it were otherwise.' It's like realism, just accepting what is or what we call 'radical acceptance' in a more clinical setting.

That radical acceptance is like, 'Yes, it happened, and now what?'

It's not hiding from it like a child, and it's not rising above it, or 'being rational,' as people might be prone to say.

What it means to be like a child in a positive way, and not a negative, is living with a childlike sense of awe, wonder, and curiosity.

Being able to navigate through uncertainty, being flexible in what we believe to be right or correct, being okay with not knowing everything, knowing that there are other people who have knowledge that you don't have, and that you can gain access to knowledge if you like.

But we will never know everything, but remaining optimistic about the outcome of things, whether that's in the interpersonal realm or in the view of the planet, keeping in mind that our technology will catch up to all the potential disastrous environmental calamities, and maintain a sense of playfulness along the way.

Let's be honest, probably about 80% of my childlike behaviors, are within the confines of my home with my wife.

The awe and the wonder I experience isn't visible when I'm walking down the street or driving down the road. Nobody knows that in my head, in my mind, I am experiencing a sense of awe, wonderment, and curiosity.

I won't stop the random person on the street and say, "What's the difference between that cloud and that cloud?"

Because clouds have names based on the different structures, sizes, and shapes. I don't know the names of all the clouds, but I love looking at them.

I remember my dad tried to teach me once,

and I said, "I don't want to know. I just want to be in wonder of clouds. I don't want to know all their names."

I don't want to have a degree in atmospheric sciences or earth sciences.

I just want to marvel at the mountains and lakes and rivers. I just want to be in awe and wonder of nature.

I don't want or need to know all the names of the differences between the lake and the stream, and the brook, and the river.

I don't need to know that to enjoy them.

———

Awe, wonder, curiosity, uncertainty, flexibility, unknowing, optimistic, playful, intuitive, trusting.

Awe-ness is looking at the big picture and thinking, 'Oh my gosh, I'm standing on a round chunk of dirt that is moving around in the galaxy's solar system.'

Wonder for me is about looking into how the solar system works.

Like, "Oh, there are other planets, there are stars and moons, and we have a sun, what's the difference between our planet and other planets."

Whereas curiosity is taking it one step further and looking for information or answers, like, "Why does Jupiter look like it does versus how Venus looks," or "What are the different proximities to the sun and the planets."

The awe is just the noticing of it, it's vastness can be overwhelming, but not in a negative way.

Some people can become teary-eyed watching a sunrise or sunset. Others can lose all sense of time watching an eagle soar through the sky, it's a magnificent thing you're witnessing.

Paradox

If you feel certain about things, if you have no sense of awe, wonder, or curiosity, then that means that you feel certain about things. Or the opposite could be that you feel entirely uncertain, and you are not happy with that.

You feel ignorant, and stupid, and you might have even been told when you were growing up that you were dumb, and not likely to achieve much.

Some people, don't experience those feelings, perhaps it's because somebody told them to knock it off because they were acting like a child, or because they somehow related experiencing awe and wonder to being naive, ignorant, dumb, or being told to get their head out of the clouds.

If you're going into relationships, getting a degree, or going into the workforce without a sense of awe, wonder, and curiosity, you are likely going to become cynical and certain about things. And then you are possibly strident in how you interact with other people.

You may become opinionated and argumentative and take a more nihilistic view of things.

And that makes people around you unhappy. Quite frankly, people don't like to be around unhappy people.

People also don't tend to prefer being around others who don't seem to have their feet firmly planted on the ground.

Again, it's that middle place between being completely untethered from reality and being chained down to the stake in the ground.

With paradox, there's not a denial of what's going on around you, but it's acting in a way that others might find puzzling given the circumstances.

But it's because you know something else. You know joy, you know happiness, you know love, you know contentment.

And so you're not easily dissuaded from those things, nor persuaded to stay in the muck. The muck exists, we can't deny the muck.

There are people doing dangerous things. There are horrible things happening to people all around the world.

There are unanswerable questions about the environmental impact of technology. But staying stuck in that mind space makes people close in, they can become 'single issue' people.

How do you have ongoing relationships with

a multitude of people if you're constantly fixated on one thing?

That's what paradox is about.

In addition to paradox, it could also be perspective. When you have perspective, you know about the goings-on that are troubling in your world, in your community. But you also know about really wonderful things going on.

And so you have a sense of perspective, which is what can help you live in this middle place.

Intuition

With intuition, we get a sense, an inkling.

If we are not attentive to the signals that our body sends us, like "I'm hungry," "I'm thirsty," or "I'm tired," if we deny those messages, our mind learns to not send those messages anymore, because we're not heeding them.

And so intuition is like that. It will send us a message. And maybe the hairs on the back of our neck will stand up, which is a signal being sent from a deep system within our brain that's telling us to be on alert and be aware. It can be a danger signal.

We have an innate neurological system that is integrated with or works in parallel with our intuition.

We go through our lives, we have experiences, we have encounters with people, and we take in information, but we can't exclusively apply that information to a current situation, or person we're engaging with, that's cognitive bias.

But the retention of past experiences gives us the ability to have an intuitive sense about the person we're encountering, the topic we're encountering, or the place that we're inhabiting.

When we do get those messages, we have to be able to discern whether they're helpful or harmful messages, and whether we're going to heed those messages or not.

But a lot of people who praise intuition seem to find that it serves them well, and I've definitely been that kind of person. I feel like I have a good sense of people. I feel like I have a good gauge of people's intentions.

If you think about it this way, children who have gone through abuse can become very adept at noticing the micro signals in people, signals that are communicating deception, contempt, and hidden rage.

They can detect all the little micro-expressions in the face. They are really tapped into the 'energy' of the room and can notice when things are heating up.

———

I was an independent contractor with a civil rights organization, and I made the decision to walk away from the organization, which most people would think is doing good things in and for the world.

I think that's largely true, but my intuition was telling me that there was also something else going on, behind the scenes, out of view of people outside the organization. It was very specific to transgender issues.

There was a particular direction the organization started to take, that was not sitting well with me. I basically wanted to get out. Nothing bad had happened. I wasn't having a conflict. I was basically being paid very well, to do good work. And it's not always the wisest thing to walk away from a secure position.

There was no other job to take its place. It's a major financial loss.

The organization had been deemed a transphobic organization by trans radical activists on social media.

But my attempt at the time was to steer the course in a better direction. I was there to keep it from going off-course. But I recognized, at a certain point, that I wasn't going to be successful. The currents were so strong that they were pushing me off course, and there was nothing I could do to correct that.

I wasn't going to be able to just push everybody over, grab the helm, and pull us back. I didn't have the authority to do it, I didn't have the bandwidth that was needed to take that task on. I kept trying, and then eventually I jumped overboard before the whole thing sank.

What I'd say about intuition is to trust but verify. Our intuition is a good signal, we should be paying attention to it, and what it's telling us. We also need to verify.

If we don't verify those messages that we're getting, then that's another form of cognitive bias. Then we are operating under a system that's based on preconceived notions or previously experienced information.

We have to be able to trust and then verify, and then if we're correct in our assumption about what's going on, or the signals we're getting are correct, then we can act accordingly.

And what we're doing is, we're teaching ourselves that the body can send us signals, our mind can send us signals, and we can trust those signals.

"Yes, I'm hungry," "Yes, I'm thirsty," "Yes, I need to pee," "Yes, that person might be dangerous," and "Yes, I might need to get out of this situation because it's not going to be good for me in the long run."

We have to start with the simplest things, which is our body just giving us the signals that it's sending us, to stay alive.

Our intuition is important because it's an internal wisdom that we have gained throughout our lifetime. Our mind is storing every experience we've ever had.

For example, if you're walking down the street at night, and you feel somebody gaining on you from behind, that's your brain sending a signal to pay attention, you might be in danger. So pay attention to that. Do what you need to do. Turn around, cross the street, or duck into a building.

Our intuition is also sending us signals. I guess you could say that that is just experiences, there might not be any reason to differentiate between the two.

The fight or flight or freeze mechanism in our brain, the limbic system, that's sending us those signals, is a very important system. It wants us to stay alive, that's its sole goal. And so intuition is just another way of talking about that.

Some people, more theistically, would say to trust in God, and that God knows the plan for you. While science would say your limbic system is sending you signals to keep you alive. So this is just like a non-theistic and non-scientific way of talking about a similar phenomenon.

Optimism

Optimism is, fundamentally, feeling hopeful about the future. The fewer complications that we encounter in our young years, the more we're able to maintain some of that optimism.

For people who have really difficult childhoods, optimism isn't as easily accessible. I believe it can be developed, but it'll come later, unless they get a stable and consistent adult in their life who is more optimistic in their frame of reference, and they can attach to that person, rather than a more nihilistic or neurotic parent.

So it's hopefulness and it's future-focus. Realism. Or reality testing is about asking 'What is the situation right now? What can I do about it?'

Pragmatism, on the other hand, is thinking about what you can practically do in the moment. It's not looking up theories and textbooks or relying on data from the research studies, it's very much centered in the here and now. Very practical.

Children tend to be very present-focused.

Children are typically not focusing on the past because there's not much of it.

And they're not thinking about the future that process comes up more in late adolescence when our prefrontal cortex is getting wired up, when we're in our late teens, early twenties for females, and mid to late twenties for males.

I was one of those people who had a tough childhood, so I wasn't optimistic as a young person.

Optimism came to me in a very forced, and almost coercive way. When I was in my early twenties, I was in a relationship with another young woman.

And she said to me one day, "You know what? You don't see the good in anything," "You're always focused on the negative."

And I was like, "What? What do you mean?" because in my reality, I didn't know what she was referring to.

And she said, "You never notice the sunsets.

You never noticed the flowers on the side of the road. You rarely smile."

We lived in San Diego, but I didn't really pay attention to the ocean. That's how bad it was. Let's just be frank.

And so she got these little stickers children have in classrooms or in homes where you're trying behavior modification. And she put little stickers on a calendar on the fridge.

If I had noticed something positive, she would put a sticker on that day. And if I got like three or four in a row, I would get a reward.

At first, I was really angry about that. Because I didn't like being treated like a child.

What it forced me to do was focus as much as I could on all the fun and positive things, because "She wasn't right about me."

And it took all of my focus, it was straining, like lifting too heavy of a weight, to start noticing and pointing out beautiful scenes and happy moments.

That was a difficult experience to go through as a 20-something-year-old, but it was also a major pivot point in my life.

What it taught me was that regardless of what

I had been through up to that point, the first 20 years of my life were not good, it didn't have to be my future.

Playfulness

Nobody's going to go skipping down the corridor in the corporate office. (Although I recommend they do. Let's get some hopscotch going on in the boardroom.)

Playfulness allows for the opportunity of brevity, bringing in humor, and not being so serious all the time. Life is a serious matter, I don't want to downplay that.

Paying the bills is not fun. And some people work in jobs that are a vocation, but not an avocation, they're not passionate about it.

I'll give you an example of how playfulness comes into my life on a very regular basis.

My wife and I hold hands when we're walking around the house. Do you know people who do that? Do you hold hands with your partner or spouse when you're just walking from the bedroom to the kitchen? It's something people may do when they're young and in love, we want to be connected to that person the whole time. And so it too can show up in a relationship where after 21 years of marriage, I want to hold my wife's hand, and she wants to hold my hand when we're walking anywhere. There might be no music playing at all, and we'll just enjoy a little dance in the dining room.

Being spontaneous is playfulness and not being worried about people thinking you're being silly, and the self-consciousness that comes with that.

It's important because if we behave according to what we believe are the dictates of others, we will be judged by them for behaving inappropriately, so to speak, we're going to stop.

There are some guardrails. There are things that we probably shouldn't do when we're in a mixed company because we will be judged harshly.

And there are lots of miserable people out there, they don't like to see people happy and in love, and so they will judge happy and loving people harshly.

But for somebody like me, I don't care. I'm like Teflon, that doesn't bother me. But for other people, that might bother them.

The people who are ultra-concerned about their own misery, and/or the misery in the world, are not going to think too kindly of people who are happy.

They'll call it 'toxic positivity.' I know what they mean, and I think they're over-projecting.

Those type of people think some people are just a bunch of fakes. Like Stewart Smalley from Saturday Night Live, who looked in the mirror, and said "I'm Good Enough, I'm Smart Enough, and Doggone It, People Like Me!".

Reciting positive affirmations in the bathroom mirror was a popular thing to do in the 80s, following the success of Louise Hay's book You Can Heal Your Life (1984, Hay House Publishing). This character made fun of it. And people still do belittle that kind of stuff. A nihilistic or strident person would cut somebody down who exhibited that kind of behavior.

You might be a person who does positive reinforcement with affirmations. You might have a little sticky note on your bathroom mirror that tells you to look at yourself and smile and say I love you. Good for you! I was raised in an environment that really appreciated positive affirmations.

It comes from my exposure to the Church of Religious Science and Unity Church, where my mom was a minister. Both denominations are in the same New Thought system. I was raised with that philosophy around.

I understand it, but it's negated as something silly, stupid, and not worthwhile. Those against "toxic positivity' say what we should really be doing is interrogating ourselves and finding all our faults.

The people who seem to mind the most, matter the least.

If I'm okay with being playful, and my wife is okay with me being playful, and I've been able to go 57 years of my life, most of them as an adult, being that way and have not been punished in any way for it, as far as I know, although I know there are people who don't like it, they don't matter to me.

We often conceal parts of ourselves for fear that we will be judged.

By whom? Do they even matter? Does a stranger, sitting next to us at the bus stop really matter? Or can we put some headphones on and dance to some music?

Who cares what they think.

Unknowing

This is where we get a little bit into the 'Eastern versus Western' ways of thinking. We prize knowing something in Western cultures. Having the right answer.

When a teacher asks you a question, you shoot your hand up, "I've got an answer for that."

Because we want to be recognized, we want to be competent.

That's how we get promotions, that's how we get rewarded, and quite honestly, that's how we attract mates in our Western culture in a lot of ways. I have, with almost every person I've been in a relationship with, except Margaret, my wife.

When I was in front of a room talking, people

were like, "Ooh, commanding the room. Good personality!"

Those are the things that people were attracted to. Because I had answers to questions.

But I didn't always. And I was really honest about that.

Unknowing is much more important in more Eastern cultures, philosophically at least. I wouldn't say that Confucianism is necessarily about the unknowing. That's how the government works. I'm talking about it more philosophically.

And so unknowing is about recognizing that we don't have all the answers. There are experiences that I haven't had, and I can't just put myself into that predicament or situation and come up with how I would respond.

We can run ourselves through visual exercises. There are a lot of people who do that all the time.

When I worked for the federal government, we had to complete training on how we would respond if an active shooter came into the building. And when I was in law enforcement, how would I respond if somebody approached me with a gun?

And even Olympic athletes do it. Because the more you can see the scenario play out in your mind, and play through all the possible situations that are occurring and how you would deal with that, then you're going to be better.

Because you're putting it in your mind, and the mind doesn't know the difference between thinking about it and experiencing it.

There's a famous story about Michael Phelps, the Olympic swimmer, who still won his race, even though his goggles were filled up with water.

One of the reasons for that is that his coach constantly had him running through visualization drills. And he said he was bored one day, and he ran a visualization based on what if water got into his goggles. So then he would know how to respond to that.

The unknowingness doesn't mean that we can't attempt to gain some perspective on things, or some possible outcomes, but we can't really know. And in our culture, not knowing, it's the opposite.

It means that we're incompetent or less competent. It means that we, generally speaking, haven't done our homework.

A lot of us go to school for many, many years. Especially just kindergarten through 12th grade.

And so we're indoctrinated into this way of thinking, "Here's the question, who's got the answer?", and the one who has the answer, especially the correct answer, is the one who gets praised in front of the whole room and people want that, they want that praise, not all the kids, but a majority.

Then those kids become adults, and they go into the workplace, they go into colleges, and they go into their relationships having to have the answer, or needing to come up with the answer, which is what often brings couples into couples therapy.

One member of the couple has a lot of questions, and the other person wants to give them the answers.

And the person with the questions is like, "No, I don't want the answers. I just want you to listen."

Here, sex doesn't really matter. The media portrays it as men having the answers and women having the questions.

My wife is a marriage and family therapist. It's just whoever is the most dominant. It doesn't matter if they're male or female. There are lots of men who want to be listened to and wives who just want to give them the answers.

So it's just a dynamic that shows up. It's really ingrained in us. We can feel stuck.

———

This is an opportunity to become unstuck.

I don't do clinical work in the psychotherapeutic sense anymore, but in the clinical work that I do as an emotional wellness and mental fitness workshop presenter, I hear it constantly.

People feel stuck, stuck in a job, stuck in a marriage, stuck in a particular role.

It's about getting unstuck.

It's an opportunity to say, "Okay, so this is what's happened so far in your life. Are you satisfied with that? Do you want more of that?"

If you don't want more of that, maybe do some self-exploration, get in there (your mind) and do some excavating or spelunking, get in there and figure out what needs to change.

'How can I change it?', 'How much do I have control over?'"

We don't have 100% control over everything in our lives. And I think that's also hard for people to recognize.

We can't control everything.

I haven't been part of a recovery community, but of course I've worked with people in recovery from drug abuse and alcoholism.

And they have the serenity prayer, and the gist of it is determining and differentiating between what I can and cannot control in my life.

Some people say, "I give up those things I can't control to God."

Some people will say, "I just accept it. And I figure out how to move through it, how to tolerate the distress, and regulate the emotions."

That's what I teach people how to do, it's going to be a different route.

It's about getting unstuck. People will say, "I don't have much choice in the matter."

We always have choice, but choice isn't easy. That's more what we mean.

This is really difficult. Welcome to adulting.

It is difficult because now you have to figure out, where you're going to move, which job you're going to take, if you're going to stay or go with this person, what you're going to do, what kind of boundaries you're going to put up in your life that says, "You know what, mom? I'm going to hang up on you every time you talk to me that way."

The way I think about it is that there are potentially more opportunities, when you occupy this third space, middle space, or whatever people are going to refer to it as.

In that space, there's a bit more breathing room. It's not so crowded, physically and metaphysically, and there's more opportunity to sit down or take a moment to consider what you want to do, how you want to do it, and how you're going to communicate it to other people.

We have to be very clear with the people when we're setting boundaries or expectations. And so it's a place to come and take a break.

There's some respite there, and the ability to step away from the more ideological, for example, with the group that you maybe hang out with on a regular basis, and you go, "You know what? I don't think I am 100% tied in with this. I'm really going to go see what those other people over there are saying from the safety of my middle place. I'm not going to join up with them, I'm not going to go shift a Green Party member to a Tea Party member."

That's not going to happen. Although I think I do know some people who have made quite a drastic shift like that.

And so it's about getting outside those systems, systems of thinking, systems of believing. People who have concerns or thoughts about their church, their house of worship, the religion it's attached to, the culture that's reinforcing the ideas, their friend network, their workplace, their school system, or their family, can take some reprieve from that.

But it's not necessarily safer, because when you're in the middle space, you get the bows and arrows from all directions.

It can actually be a bit more dangerous, but you can gain a sense of competence and confidence in knowing that you are making up your own mind about things and that you've done your due diligence in observing, reading, and running through scenarios.

And so you're going to put a big shield around you so those bows and arrows will be able to bounce off .

But you have to build that up, you have to have that resiliency, and the capacity for that resiliency, and you have to have the tools and strategies with which you can build that resilience with.

I look forward to seeing and meeting you in the third space.

We can be childlike there.

CONCLUSION

There's not much that we can do individually, and even collectively in some cases,
to eradicate all the misery in the world. But
we sure do have the ability to not add to it.

So stop adding to the misery, your own, your
family's, your workplace's, your community's,
your country's, your planet's.

Stop adding to the misery.

The saying is 'misery loves company.' It sure
is true. But it doesn't have to be about you.

There's so much beauty out in the world.
Beautiful people, beautiful places, beautiful
experiences.

When you're feeling low, look up.

Literally. Raise your face up.

Look up to the ceiling, to the sky, and smile a big smile.

Even if it's a fake smile. It releases hormones into your brain and into your body to make you feel better. It's just something that happens.

We spend too much time focused on looking down, literally. Watch people when you're walking down the street. How many people are looking at the sidewalk while they're walking? They don't even trust that they're going to walk without falling. They don't want to make eye contact with people. People aren't even looking straight ahead.

When I'm walking around, I'm looking up and around all the time.

I'm looking in the trees.

I'm looking for squirrels.

I'm looking up in the clouds.

I'm fascinated by all that nature has displayed. That's that awe and wonder.

I don't want to put more misery into the world, there's enough already, it doesn't need mine.

Really difficult, tragic things that would probably land people in jail now, happened to me in the first 20 years of my life.

The one truth that I've come to from all of that experience is that it made me who I am today.

And so when people say, "If you could go back and redo your childhood, would you?", I always say no. Because I really like where I've landed, and I don't know where I would have landed otherwise.

I would hate to relive those things. I liked that I stopped experiencing those things in my 20s and went on from there, rather than dealing with it into my 30s.

Find a way to embrace all the hardships. Find the lesson, find the learning in the hardships. And let people go. Forgive them for your own sake.

Stop that need to defame people or destroy people, like so many people do now on social media by trying to malign people's character.

Forgiveness might not be possible for some, but I'd say at least attempt it. Spend the rest of your life attempting to forgive people.

At least let go of the anger and the resentment, because the longer you keep that connection, the longer that person or those people or that system, have control over you. They're winning.

There's a technique used in some types of psychotherapy where you sit a person in a chair, then you sit an empty chair across from them, and you have them imagine a person is there, a person they hold resentment for, and they have a conversation with that person. They may even shout at the invisible person.

Sometimes the therapist knows the story of your life well enough that they can play the character of that other person in the discussion.

Right now, I could put a chair in front of me and imagine my paternal grandmother, who's the most evil woman, and have a conversation that isn't charged with a bunch of raw emotions.

That's because I spent time in my late twenties and early thirties working through all those feelings. And, I learned things her life and her struggles and her challenges. That doesn't excuse what she did, but I have a better understanding of what made her such a harsh and cruel person.

I've never done that chair exercise personally. But I could do it because I've done things similar to that.

I know a lot of people who are striving for a middle-place existence.

They say, "It's always out of grasp."

I'd say, "Look at all of the resentments, all of the grudges, all of the lack of forgiveness, all of the expectations of others, all of the unspoken, unwritten, unverbalized taboos or expectations. Look at all of those things and just systematically let them go."

I think starting with the self is a good spot. Letting go of whatever traps, restraints, or boxes, that we have put ourselves into, that happened from before we had consciousness of what we were doing. Limits that were fed into, and we've carried the burdens with us.

So get those keys out and start opening up all those doors, open the cuffs, and let things go.

Learn how to joyfully make mistakes and laugh.

Laugh at your faults.

We don't want to be insecure, but we also don't want to tie ourselves up into knots searching for some type of impenetrable security, either.

We have to figure out how to be okay with the fact that sometimes we're going to do the wrong thing, say the wrong thing, be in the wrong place. We'll deal with it when that happens.

There are people who are so afraid of that, that they literally don't leave their homes. My wife has a client like that. She hasn't left her home in over a decade.

We do that. We either lock ourselves in our homes or surround ourselves with all these different belongings, like hoarders who have boxes and piles of things all around them.

We surround ourselves with a bunch of people who tell us what we want to hear. We insulate ourselves from the pain and discomfort of life, but there is no escape.

That's the lesson that Siddhartha, the Buddha, came to realize. That there is no escape from suffering.

There is only suffering, but how do we respond to that suffering?

We can hide ourselves, like his family did, behind their walls. Or we can do what he did when he spent time with the Jains sitting under the tree with one little piece of clothing, eating what people gave him as he was begging for food.

As I spoke about earlier in the book, Buddhism is the middle path between the denial of self in Jainism, and the overindulgence in the self as he experienced in his family's Hindu Brahmin class.

So the middle path, the third space, is about learning how to deal with, navigate through, suffering, uncertainties and unknowings.

I feel like I've demonstrated, through my life, that I say and do what I need to say and do.

I can be considered controversial, but I have

friends who have been friends of mine for many years and when people say, "You're friends with Zander? Why are you friends with Zander?"

They'll say things like, "Because he's loyal. Because he cares. Because he listens to me, he encourages me. He's a champion for whatever I'm working on."

Anybody who knows me has had that experience. And those who haven't met me can glean who I am, through reading this book.

———

Please do all you can to free yourself from the restrictions, the confines, that limit your life.

Do all you can to free yourself, and then teach other people how you did that.

I feel like that's what I've done, I've learned how to do things, and now I'm teaching people how they can do things.

And just one last thing:

Love yourself enough to take charge of your life.

ABOUT THE AUTHOR

Social Worker, public speaker, educator, and podcast host Zander Keig, renowned for his impactful presentations, has earned many distinguishing accolades, including the 2020 National Social Worker of the Year award from the National Association of Social Workers (NASW) and the 2018 Social Worker of the Year award from the NASW California Chapter.

Zander is the founder of Keig Consulting, a veteran of the U.S. Coast Guard, and a first-generation American of Mexican heritage (Latino) trans man with subject matter expertise in social care, spiritual discernment, and mental fitness, and the host of the Umbrella Hour Podcast on the UK Health radio network.

"The Third Space: A Nonconformist's Guide to the Universe turns every reader into an expert locksmith by providing them with the ultimate master key that unlocks the doors they once thought were shut to them in their lives."

— **Daryl Davis**, Musician, Author, Race Reconciliator

ABOUT THE AUTHOR

Social worker, public speaker, educator, and podcast host Zander Keig, renowned for his impactful presentations, has earned many distinguishing accolades, including the 2020 National Social Worker of the Year award from the National Association of Social Workers (NASW) and the 2018 Social Worker of the Year award from the NASW California Chapter.

Zander is the founder of Keig Consulting, a veteran of the U.S. Coast Guard, and a first-generation American of Mexican heritage (Latino) trans man with subject matter expertise in social care, spiritual discernment, and mental fitness, and the host of the Umbrella Hour Podcast on the UK Health radio network.

Thought Leader Press

ISBN 978-1-61343-169-6